SUGARCANE ACADEMY

ALSO BY MICHAEL TISSERAND

The Kingdom of Zydeco

ADVANCE PRAISE FOR
Sugarcane Academy

"Michael Tisserand knows more about life in New Orleans than anybody else I know. *Sugarcane Academy* is a poignant, well-written, and awe-inspiring nonfiction saga of Louisiana citizens coping with Katrina's wrath. Highly recommended."

> —Douglas Brinkley, professor of history at Tulane University
> and author of *The Great Deluge*

"Hurricane Katrina was a predatory beast with many mouths, and it mauled, devoured, and disrupted lives across the spectrum of society. *Sugarcane Academy* is the story of how one resourceful group of families found a way to maintain their sense of community, and their commitment to a future for their children, through a difficult exile. It is also a moving portrait of a teacher with a true vocation, and a reminder of what that vocation can, and must, mean if we hope to heal our wounded society."

> —Tom Piazza, author of *Why New Orleans Matters*

"With his sharp eye for detail and his abundant heart, Tisserand paints a devastating portrait of the toll exacted by Hurricane Katrina, particularly on the children. Simple, compelling, and quietly dramatic, *Sugarcane Academy* is both eulogy and commencement—a tribute to the endurance of the human spirit."

> —Mike Sager, writer-at-large, *Esquire*

"In the aftermath of Katrina, Paul Reynaud and these families courageously forged ahead, rather than lingering upon what might once have been done. As we consider the future of New Orleans there's much to learn from their inspiring lesson."

> —Chris Mooney, author of *The Republican War on Science*
> and *Storm World: Hurricanes, Politics, and*
> *the Battle Over Global Warming*

SUGARCANE ACADEMY

*How a New Orleans Teacher
and His Storm-Struck Students
Created a School to Remember*

Michael Tisserand

A Harvest Original
Harcourt, Inc.
Orlando Austin New York San Diego Toronto London

Requests for permission to make copies of
any part of the work should be submitted online at
www.harcourt.com/contact or mailed to the following address:
Permissions Department, Harcourt, Inc.,
6277 Sea Harbor Drive, Orlando, Florida 32887-6777.

www.HarcourtBooks.com

Library of Congress Cataloging-in-Publication Data
Tisserand, Michael, 1963–
Sugarcane Academy: how a New Orleans teacher
and his storm-struck students created a school to remember/
Michael Tisserand.—1st ed.
p.   cm.
1. Education—Louisiana—New Orleans.   2. Hurricane
Katrina, 2005—Social aspects.   3. Environmental refugees—
Education (Elementary)—Louisiana—New Orleans.   I. Title.
LA297.N4T77   2007
372.9763'35—dc22   2006030414
ISBN 978-0-15-603189-9

Text set in Bembo
Designed by Lydia D'moch

Printed in the United States of America
First edition
A C E G I K J H F D B

To Mr. R.
and all the teachers

PROLOGUE

~~~~~~

Our first-ever attempt to board up a house was on a Monday morning in mid-September 2004. Hurricane Ivan had hit Grenada and pinballed around the Gulf of Mexico until it headed our way. I'd lived in New Orleans for the better part of twenty years and had once driven into the path of a hurricane—Hurricane Andrew in 1992—to cover the storm as a journalist from a hotel room in the town of New Iberia. The wind peeled off the hotel roof, and I filed the story for *USA Today*. But I'd never tried to prepare my own home for a storm.

My wife, Tami, and I had purchased the house six months earlier, in the spring of 2004. It was down the block from Lusher Elementary School, our favorite public school in New Orleans. We had two young children. It was time to take hurricanes more seriously.

So we drove to the hardware store and purchased two pieces of plywood, each roughly the size of a twin bedsheet. For the next hour, we tried to affix the boards to the face of our porch to cover a window. It went badly. A borrowed handsaw lodged in the wood and bent. I cursed and heaved the plywood sheet across the front lawn, providing comic relief for the people driving past our house on their way out of town.

We gave up. The sound of a table saw drew us across the street to a neighbor's backyard. He was wearing a sweat-soaked T-shirt and cutoffs. He looked at us, poured himself a vodka, and plucked a pencil from behind his ear. "Measure twice, cut once," he said.

When finally the porch was boarded up, we put out enough food to last our cats for a few days. Then we got on the highway, found our place in the slow-moving dismissal of the city, and drove to the home of our friends, Scott and Cindy Jordan, in the Southwest Louisiana town of Carencro. Ivan took a turn away from New Orleans, and after a couple fun days in Carencro we returned home. I went back to my job as editor of *Gambit Weekly,* a local newspaper. My wife went back to her part-time job as a doctor at Treadway Pediatrics, a local, family-run firm. The kids went back to school.

"All you ever wanted was to marry Tami and live in New Orleans," a friend once told me, and she was mostly right. I met my wife in 1983, when we were both freshmen at Northwestern University in Evanston, Illinois. I left that program when I was a sophomore and hitchhiked to see Mardi Gras in New Orleans, a city that had fascinated me since the summer before I turned sixteen years old, when my father drove my cousin and me to New Orleans for a vacation. That year, my dad got sick and was confined to the hotel room; liberated like never before, I found my way to Preservation Hall, a legendary French Quarter jazz club that allows minors inside. I sat at the feet of old musicians and was kept spellbound as Kid Thomas Valentine and Sweet Emma Barrett sang about Li'l Liza Jane and Basin Street and the St. James Infirmary. I'd never seen or heard anything like it. On that same trip, Hurricane Bob passed near New Orleans and my cousin and I went running across stone sidewalks through a shuttered French Quarter, pitching back and forth in the high winds like drunken sailors.

Through the years, New Orleans kept calling. Long after my hitchhiking journey, I returned yet again to the city. It was the late 1980s. Tami was taking premed classes at the University of New Orleans, and I started working as a music journalist, a pursuit that Tami had first suggested to me while we sat on a balcony in our rented Uptown apartment. We moved around a bit more; she eventually went to medical school in Wisconsin, where our first child, Cecilia, was born. Then in 1998, I once more talked Tami into moving to New Orleans. I got the job at the newspaper, and she started work as a pediatrician. We were in our late thirties and had careers and a mortgage. I thought we were finally there to stay.

Then on Friday, August 26, 2005, nearly one year after our Ivan evacuation, I learned that another hurricane was turning toward New Orleans. Tami was on call that weekend, so she had gone to bed early. After watching the ten o'clock news, I woke her up to tell her that the kids and I might be evacuating to Carencro the next day.

This time we were efficient; we had the old plywood, still cleanly sized. We put it up first thing Saturday morning. The kids chose stuffed animals for the drive. Tami packed their clothes. She had to stay in town to receive calls from patients. The next morning, she was on duty to visit the hospitals to check on newborn babies. If the storm looked bad, we decided, she'd retreat to the offices of the daily newspaper, the *Times-Picayune*. A friend worked there, and she'd remain with him at the paper until it all blew over.

Our evacuation settled on, I stopped following the news. I had no idea that it was already predicted that the city's levee system might fail, that Lake Pontchartrain's water might pour into New Orleans, that thousands could die, that more than a million people might be driven from their homes. Of course, I had some sense of the risk. Both the local paper and national magazines had proclaimed the likelihood of such a tragedy. The previous year, my own newspaper had published a cover story titled "Disaster in the Making," which detailed the crippling of the Federal Emergency Management Agency. But I couldn't recall looking at the headline and feeling all that uneasy for my adopted home. It was just another story.

Even that last weekend of August, when I heard that a hurricane named Katrina was coming our way, I mostly thought about the new school year. Cecilia had flown through the first days of second grade at Lusher Elementary. Her teacher, Megan Neelis, was so naturally affectionate that some kids called her Teddy. We'd signed Cecilia up for her second year in the school's dance troupe, a wonderful program in which I'd witnessed the music and magic of New Orleans that first drew me there. I wondered if this might be the year when my kid danced in the city's Jazz Fest.

Our four-year-old son, Miles, the only New Orleans native in the family, had just one more year before he'd attend his big sister's school. He couldn't wait. Neither could we. It was almost September. Even the summer's heat would soon fade.

Despite the mayor's call for a voluntary evacuation, I was in no hurry to leave. Around lunchtime on Saturday, while I placed our suitcases into the trunk, Cecilia looked down Lowerline Street toward her school. She saw a familiar gray Toyota Corolla parked in front. Her first-grade teacher was working over the weekend. "I'm going down to Mr. Reynaud's," Cecilia shouted over her shoulder, not waiting for my response. She knew I'd say yes. It had become our Saturday routine.

Cecilia's previous year in Mr. Reynaud's class still glowed inside her. One evening, I watched as she drew a red heart and the name "Mr. R" on a piece of paper. When I looked over, she quickly crossed it out. But my daughter wasn't the only ex–first grader who kept returning to the old classroom after school and on weekends. Paul Reynaud had a knack for making kids feel like they were right where they belonged. He was a man in his fifties with quick eyes, a close-cropped salt-and-pepper beard, a half-dozen pens and pencils always in the right pocket of a button–down shirt, and a playground whistle where other men knotted their neckties. He seemed to live in the school.

I watched Cecilia enter the familiar schoolyard, then I turned up another street to check on neighbors. This past year, we'd taken to walking to school with two other families who lived up Plum Street. Chris Poche and Georgia Flynn were a block away, in a lavender house behind a chain–link fence, with their three sons: Eli, a first grader; Adam, who was in preschool; and Owen, just learning to talk. Another half block away lived the Hustons. Derek and Kiki Huston's oldest child was Olivia, a fourth grader and a lifelong friend of Cecilia's. Walker was in first grade, and Callie was in preschool. On weekday mornings, when the combined families rounded our corner on their walk to school, they'd call on us to join them. We'd hurry on shoes. At full strength, our sleepy mob totaled six adults and seven kids.

The Poches and the Hustons already had planned to stay together in St. Martinville for the evacuation, just as they had for Ivan. Last year, we all met up at Dean-O's, a restaurant in Lafayette that specializes in crawfish pizza. The back room was filled with our friends and others who had evacuated. "New Orleans in the house!" we shouted. Then, our favorite neighborhood story was about how Derek Huston had stayed behind and set off the Poches' alarm by going after some beer in their refrigerator.

Now, as Katrina churned in the Gulf, the Poches had gone ahead to beat the evacuation traffic. With Tami staying home and Derek in Washington, D.C., for a funeral, I checked in with Kiki. We decided to caravan our way out of town.

I walked the block back to my house. The scene in our kitchen mimicked any other Saturday. Tami was on the phone, calming a mother whose child had a mild fever. She rolled her eyes at me as she repeated familiar words of medical advice. Miles sat at the counter, drawing circles on paper. He chose a new piece of paper for each circle.

Feeling restless, I went back to the school.

Inside Paul's classroom, picture books spilled off shelves. A Brueghel print was taped on one wall. Cardboard planets and kids' art hung from the ceiling with string and paper clips. Looking around, I imagined you could have peeled back the layers of clutter in this room to uncover artifacts from Paul's first year of teaching.

Cecilia and her former teacher were sitting at a computer, playing a game that seemed to involve race cars. When I walked in, Paul had a hand raised in the air as if he was cheering for himself. He must have won a race.

We talked about the storm. He didn't expect to leave. His parents, both in their eighties, had no plans to go. They were all lifelong New Orleanians who never evacuated, he said.

I looked around the room at the bank of computers along the wall, at desks and chairs clustered together for study groups, at drawings of make-believe Mardi Gras floats. Beneath the windows were a dingy throw rug and an old couch for reading time. You could just sink into this room. It was like New Orleans that way.

But the traffic lines out of town were getting longer, the highways more crowded. I knew that Kiki wanted to get on the road.

"Okay," I said to Cecilia. "Let's go." We said good-bye to Paul. Just like that, we left.

CHAPTER 1

The neighborhood kept its Sunday date for lunch in Lafayette just as we had the previous year. We sat at a long table in the back and ordered crawfish and crabmeat pizzas, and a few pitchers of beer.

The kids were ecstatic to be together. They drew on place mats, downed their pizza and plastic cupfuls of lemonade, and hovered over video games. Their parents caught one another up on the events of the past day. I said that Tami had called that morning. There was fear in her voice. She had decided not to spend the storm with our friend at the newspaper office. She told me how he had warned her, "You need to be thinking that if you don't leave, you might be here for a while."

So she completed her hospital rounds and checked in on the newborn babies. She cleaned our house and emptied our refrigerator. Then she put our cats in the back of the car, and at about noon, she drove off toward Carencro.

I couldn't call her; she didn't have her cell phone. She didn't have her glasses. All I knew was that she was somewhere along Highway 90, a southern route that curved along the Louisiana coastline before bending north toward Lafayette.

Nobody talked about the possibility that we weren't going home anytime soon. It was as if we had already started thinking about our lives on a day-to-day basis. Later, this habit would become hard to break.

"Tami won't get stranded," I said, mostly to myself. There was a line of cars out there. Someone would help her if she needed it. Plus, I could always get in my car and head toward New Orleans and meet her.

The waitress looked over at us. Our kids were running around unchecked. We should rein them in. Nobody made a move.

"Tami will be fine," I heard someone say.

"The Volvo needs work," I replied.

Behind the bar, a television displayed a swirl of clouds that had grown monstrously large. A Category Five hurricane. We listened as the National Weather Service reported that New Orleans could be uninhabitable for weeks.

The news reports infiltrated our conversations. We talked about where we all were staying. We glanced at images of people lining up to enter the Superdome. Cameras panned over their faces. I searched to see if there were any people we knew.

"Georgia's mom is still in the hospital in New Orleans, in

intensive care," I heard someone say. I looked at Georgia. She'd been crying.

All we could do was wait.

We left the pizza place and made the half-hour drive back to Scott and Cindy's. It was about two o'clock on Sunday afternoon. Just the previous evening when we arrived in Carencro, it still felt like a normal family visit, when we might hit a Cajun music club or bring the kids to a local festival. Scott and Cindy Jordan's neighborhood isn't far from the old Evangeline Downs racetrack, where races were launched by a Cajun French-speaking announcer who shouted, "Ils Sont Partis!" Nearby is the home of the musician Buckwheat Zydeco, the accordion-playing leader of the Ils Sont Partis zydeco band. Scott and Cindy moved here from New Orleans a few years back and surrounded themselves with this local culture. They told us about how their two young sons, Evan and Quinn, gathered pecans from backyard trees and rode Big Wheels down wide country roads to visit horse farms.

We pulled out a sofa bed in their living room. Cecilia and Miles climbed in. Along with a coworker from my paper and another family and their baby, we set up kitchen chairs to form a small theater around the television. We started watching. Whether it was cable news, network news, or the Weather Channel, it was all the same show. Wind and water and predictions of landfall.

I don't remember if we first saw the lights or heard the engine. At about nine o'clock, Tami pulled into the driveway. She was shaken after nine hours in stop-and-go traffic. We carried our three cats into a back bathroom, past Scott and Cindy's three dogs. I brought out Styrofoam containers of leftover pizza, and Tami joined us in front of the television.

We watched repeats of Mayor Ray Nagin's Sunday-morning declaration of a mandatory evacuation: "Ladies and gentlemen, this is not a test. This is the real deal." The swirl of clouds drew closer to the edge of land. In replays, the knot of wind and rain advanced and stopped with a jerk, like a muscle tensing and releasing.

After sleeping a few hours on Sunday night, we awoke Monday morning and thought that the worst was over. The eye of the hurricane had missed New Orleans, passing to the east. We'd later learn that the city was hit by a fast-moving Category Three storm. The levee system was supposed to hold against such a force. We thought we might be home by the end of that week.

A computer sat in the foyer, right in front of a miniature train track where Scott and Cindy's younger son played. The adults took turns in front of the screen. I checked my e-mails and found dozens of messages from friends and family, and even more from people I hadn't heard from in years. I clicked on name after name, then got up to allow others on the computer. We relaxed a little, making lunches for the kids and taking long walks around the neighborhood.

By the next morning, we knew that rising water was filling houses in New Orleans. People woke up in second-floor bedrooms to find the contents of their lives floating on the first floor. They climbed onto rooftops. At night, some neighborhoods lit up in constellations of flashlights.

Nobody in the house really ate or slept much on Tuesday, Wednesday, and Thursday. Scott and Cindy's phone no longer worked; all lines were jammed. Cell phones stopped working, too. Carencro became an island. Cars lined the driveway, but they couldn't take us home.

At some point we discovered text messaging on our cell phones. It worked, even when we couldn't make calls. We sent and received the same message to everyone we knew: "R U OK?"

We're okay.

We tallied the names of those we couldn't reach. The Saturday we left, Tami had spoken on the phone with a friend who was about to have her first baby. She had called to ask Tami's advice about evacuating. Tami had assured her that the hospitals were the safest places in the city. "I can't believe I told her that," Tami now said. On Wednesday, we learned by e-mail that our friend and her new baby had somehow gotten out of the flooded city. Then a new name rose to the top of the list of unknowns: seven-year-old Yerema Yosipiv and his family. Cecilia had played in their home from the time she was a one-year-old. Yerema and Cecilia grew up like brother and sister. "He's my first friend," Cecilia had often said. During evacuations, Yerema's father, a doctor, routinely took his family to Tulane University Hospital. Tami and I realized they must all still be there. Weeks later, we learned that the Yosipivs were airlifted from the hospital roof, after spending several nights wondering if they would survive the ordeal.

The news from home was gruesome, and we started keeping the children away from the television. We flipped over the newspapers so they couldn't see the pictures on the front page. Stories were of mobs of people rushing the hospitals for drugs; of murders and rapes and shootings. It would take months to sort out what was rumor and what was fact. Even though I was a journalist, it took a great effort not to automatically believe the worst. Fear acted like a contagion.

On Thursday, I finally heard a firsthand account from New Orleans. An e-mail appeared on the computer from Keith Spera, my friend who worked as the music critic at the daily newspaper, the person with whom Tami almost stayed during the storm. He wrote: "It's the most horrific scene you can imagine. Where is the aid? Where is the military? Thousands of people at the convention center have received nothing—no food, no water, no instructions, no authority—for three days. Bodies lying in the street uncollected—it's inconceivable that this is happening in the United States. I interviewed so many poor, elderly and frail people trying to make their way from Central City to the convention center. Many simply will not make it."

At one point, Scott remarked, it all felt like one long day. It also was permeated by a nightmarish logic; we felt surrounded by danger. One morning, as Scott and I drove into town to get food, we saw a truck collide with a car. An old woman was driving the car. Blood poured down the side of her face. Scott jumped out and ran to her car. He cradled her, talked with her, wiped away the blood. I called 911.

On Friday, September 2, a bus carrying evacuees out of New Orleans flipped over, killing one man instantly. This happened just a few miles from us.

In Scott and Cindy's neighborhood in Carencro and in other small towns around us, some locals sprung into action, assembling a rescue brigade. They drove as close to New Orleans as they could get. Then they launched their flat-bottomed fishing boats into sunken neighborhoods, where they hovered like airplanes just above submerged cars, docking at rooftops. They saved thousands of lives without official sanction, sometimes in violation of orders to stay away. We knew a first-year medical student who wrote his father about realizing that he could— and needed to—just drive past the authorities. "The only question was right or left to get around them," he told his father in a letter. "It was the only way we could get anything done."

Help started pouring in for us, too. My old high school French teacher sent a check. A friend sent me a laptop.

Neighbors were cooking enough food to feed the four house-holds that were now making an indefinite home at Scott and Cindy's. On one of our first evenings, a couple pulled over a red wagon filled with covered dishes. They set up a five-course meal of salad, smothered steak, rice and gravy, cabbage and sausage, and bread pudding.

On Wednesday, another neighbor brought over her daughter's old purple bicycle. When we first arrived in Carencro on Saturday—back when we imagined this would be another country vacation—Cecilia told me that she was ready to learn to ride a bike. We had spent the summer practicing in Audubon Park but not getting very far. She now viewed the smooth roads leading to a horse farm and decided it was time.

Cecilia and I went outside in the warm evening. We were exhausted. Sharing a cold, we spoke in hoarse voices. Taking the lead, she asked me to hold the bike straight and then pushed down on the right pedal. She fell over on her side. Then she tried again. The third time, she was up and going. I ran alongside her for a bit. Then I stopped and stood there in this strange neighborhood and watched her ride off into the evening.

"Awesome!" she called out as I burst into tears.

Within a day of the levee break, the *Times-Picayune's* Web site had transformed into a virtual bulletin board. People posted messages about their searches for friends and family members. The board was divided by neighborhoods. At night,

I would read pleas from neighbors up and down my street who were asking for anyone who could to check on a father who was alone, or a great-aunt who was diabetic. I tried to picture their houses in my mind.

By the end of the first week the city remained flooded, and we didn't know if we still had jobs. We heard that it could be six to nine months before anyone could go back to New Orleans to live. There was no water, no electricity, and the phrase "toxic gumbo" was popping up to describe the postflood environment.

On Tuesday, my wife had gotten ahold of Kent Treadway, the head of her practice, a lifelong pediatrician and native of New Orleans. For Tami, getting a job at Treadway Pediatrics had been like receiving a ticket into the local culture. Kent and his wife, Tyra, ran the practice like an extension of their living room, where patients were seen between lengthy discussions about this year's Mardi Gras costume. Kent had inherited the family practice from his father and planned to pass it on to his own son. Hundreds, maybe thousands, of family photos of patients lined the hallways, stretching back decades and generations.

"I don't know if we're going to have a practice to come back to," Kent now told Tami, summing up the despair we all felt. "What families will return to the city with their children?"

"Did you see this?" Tami asked me one morning. In her hands was a yellow-bound book. She had brought it with her

from New Orleans. About a month before Katrina, Miles had recited a story and she had written it down. The title was "Miles and the Sun," and the story went like this:

One spring day, Miles came out of his house in New Orleans. The sun was happy to see Miles. The sun was wearing sunglasses. Miles moved to his new house and the sun got very very hot. Now it was even hotter! A fearful wild storm came with lots of monsters. Luckily, Miles wasn't in it. The water splashed all over.

The pages were filled with deep, hard-pressed scribbles that he'd made with blue and green pencils.

"I'm getting pretty bored of not having school," Cecilia told us at the end of the first week.

A children's museum in Lafayette was offering free admission to evacuees. On Friday, September 2, we met there with the Poches, the Hustons, and a few other friends we'd found in the area. There was a pretend café. The kids put on aprons and served us plastic food. As they bustled about, we sat in tiny metal chairs and talked about who was safe and who wasn't, who was staying in Louisiana and who was moving on.

Tami told us about her trip into town to register Cecilia for the Lafayette Parish school system. When she arrived at the administrative office, she saw coolers filled with water bottles and people sitting at tables with stacks of forms. She didn't know if it was the kindness or the efficiency, but she could barely speak through her tears.

Within a week of the storm, the Lafayette school system absorbed about three thousand new students. As part of the registration effort, school officials walked through the Cajundome, the city's largest sports arena, where thousands of evacuees were sheltered. I later spoke with Ouida Forsythe, who worked for the schools. She recalled meeting a five-year-old girl there. "I asked her where she was from," Ouida remembered. "She said, 'Well, I used to be from New Orleans, but I'm not anymore.' Then she looked at her mama and said, 'Where are we from?'"

What did it now mean for any of us to be a New Orleanian? Where was our city? Was it somewhere back in the floodwaters, or was it now rolling through towns like Lafayette and Houston and Dallas, in the wake of those who had fled?

I started writing a series of reports for the Association of Alternative Newsweeklies, a national organization of newspapers that included *Gambit Weekly*. I wrote the first article on Tuesday, August 30, after getting a call from the association president, who over the years had become a friend. The reporting work gave me a chance to drive around the area and visit other New Orleanians. I found myself frequently driving past the Cajundome, just to glimpse my fellow evacuees who lingered outside its walls.

At Scott's house, we offered to spell each other and watch all the kids, so we could take turns being by ourselves. We passed along tips on how to apply for food stamps and money from the Red Cross. A drive-through food bank for evacuees was staffed by convicts in striped uniforms. We set alarms for three A.M., the only time you could get through to FEMA.

We couldn't stay like this for long. Whatever else had happened, it was still September. The school year had already started, and our children needed to be enrolled somewhere.

But at the museum, as we watched the kids move from the pretend grocery store to a pretend TV studio to a pretend ambulance, splitting them up became unthinkable. We kept talking until an idea formed: We'd stay together. We'd make up our own school. We had our kids. We knew we could find more. All we needed was a teacher.

I thought I knew where I might find one.

CHAPTER 2

Paul Reynaud stayed in New Orleans through Saturday, August 27, while cars passed by his classroom on the way out of town. By late afternoon, lines of traffic had merged in the contraflow plan, in which all lanes flowed outward, pumping residents like blood from the heart of the city. An exodus had begun. But in Paul's classroom, classical music, not the newscast, was playing on the radio.

There was work to be done. At Lusher as well as across the rest of New Orleans, the new school year had a rough start. The state had rated 65 percent of the city's public schools academically unacceptable. The FBI had agents in the school district office to weed out corruption. The district announced it was slicing another $48 million from an already tight budget. At Lusher, a kindergarten-through–eighth-grade school, staff positions and programs were in jeopardy. In the first days of the new school year, parents and teachers had voted to apply for charter-school status in an effort to cushion the school from the problems of the district. All summer, in addition to tutoring students who needed extra help, Paul had worked on cutting and pasting hundreds of pages of school curricula into one long document, as part of the charter application.

Paul kept working on the project through Saturday night. At about ten thirty P.M., he locked his classroom door and drove to the carriage house located behind his parents' home. This had been his home since he was a kid. Like his classroom, it was crammed thick with books. He went to sleep without checking the news. Evacuation couldn't have been further from his mind.

When he awoke Sunday morning, he sensed the change in the air. Both he and the house had been through hurricanes before. The family went without power for a week after Hurricane Betsy in 1965. His parents were now in their eighties, however. No electricity, no sewage—these were more than inconveniences. When his mother and father returned home from early morning Mass, he would talk them into packing their bags. It wouldn't be easy.

Paul and a brother sat their parents down. "I think this is the one where we have to leave," they said.

The parents wouldn't have it.

Things went back and forth for a while. Finally, the elder Reynauds agreed to leave if there was a mandatory evacuation. At nine thirty A.M., Mayor Ray Nagin called for the evacuation. Paul then asked a childhood friend, Mary Tutwiler, if the family could retreat to her home in New Iberia, a bayou town of about 33,000 people located about 135 miles west of New Orleans, and about an hour's drive south from Carencro. Mary and her husband lived in a house on Main Street that in the 1880s had served as New Iberia's first kindergarten. Property in New Iberia is divided into lots that each face a strip of the Bayou Teche; behind the Tutwiler house, a narrow strip of field led to the bayou's muddy banks. This meant that there was running room for the Reynauds' dog, Lulu. After Paul's parents learned that there was a place for their dog, they agreed to go.

On their way out of town, they stopped by Lusher so Paul could pick up the school curriculum he'd been working on. Then they all merged into the westward line of slow-moving traffic. They followed the arc south and arrived in New Iberia by sundown, where they were joined by others—including Mary's elderly parents, who also lived in New Orleans. Mary's father was eighty-two, had heart troubles, and required a breathing machine.

The winds grew harder in New Orleans. Paul had once run a catering company with Mary; by the time he arrived with his parents and brother, a pot of duck and andouille-sausage gumbo was simmering on the stove. The families gathered around a long wooden table in the center of the house. It was Sunday night.

A rainstorm settled over New Iberia the next day. Paul caught up on his reading and mainly thought about the work that waited for him back in the classroom. On Tuesday, Mary, a journalist, went to Lafayette to do some work at the *Independent,* the weekly newspaper where Scott Jordan served as editor. By the time Mary returned, everyone in the house fully knew the extent of the flooding in New Orleans. "There was chaos," Mary recalled. "And in response to this—and this is Paul's response, I believe, to adversity—he started cooking."

Mary and Paul began each day that first week after the storm by discussing at length the evening's menu. They'd carefully shop for ingredients and purchase wine by the caseload. "We were drinking and eating as well as we possibly could, and all the time we were horrified," Mary said.

That is how it went in New Iberia. Paul followed the news from New Orleans. He tried to make his parents as comfortable as possible. For the first September in nearly two decades, he wasn't teaching.

Paul Reynaud was the third oldest in a family of eight. His father, a petroleum engineer, worked for a wildcat drilling firm and was stationed in New Iberia when Paul was born in 1955. The family moved around Louisiana and Texas but eventually returned to New Orleans.

It was a large family, accustomed to both grand celebrations and unexpected sorrows. Three of Paul's brothers died when they were in their twenties. Two were accidents and the third, the family assumes, was a murder. The body was never found.

As a young child, surrounded by a pack of brothers, Paul would romp on the beach on the Mississippi coastline, making sand sculptures of nude women, his friend Richard Hart recalled. They would also make elaborate decorations on Mardi Gras truck floats at Mary Tutwiler's house and go to horror-movie double features. "He was always the smartest kid in the class. I always sat next to him and always got into trouble, and he never did," Richard remembered.

When Paul was growing up, his primary complaint was that he never had enough time to read. Only at school could he sit with a book for as long as he desired. He also vividly remembered each of his elementary school teachers. "I liked the whole experience of school and having your little job to do," Paul said. Some of the nuns at his parochial school deserved their nickname, Sisters of No Mercy. Looking back, he believed that some just didn't care much for children. That wasn't the case with his kindergarten teacher, though.

"I really liked kindergarten," he said. "They still had this old Victorian building which was the convent. I loved how you went in this little door and down the little hall, and you got to the kindergarten room, which was bright and lively. And of the four kindergarten teachers, mine was the youngest. I thought she was beautiful.

"She was unflappable. Things would happen, people crying or throwing things. Now, kids throw a crayon and you get all bent out of shape. But back then, kids would really swat each other.

"But she had all this stuff for us to do. Go write your name. Go write it more neatly. It was all interesting and fun. From the perspective of now, they were all just sort of perfectly plain, ordinary teachers who were just doing the job."

Paul came from a longtime New Orleans restaurant family. His mother's grandfather, Lawrence Fabacher, was a well-known restaurateur who had owned Jax Brewery, in the French Quarter. Paul started cooking, and by high school he was preparing multicourse dinners for fun. When he returned to New Orleans after earning a degree in comparative literature at Columbia University, he started working in restaurants. His plan was to earn some money before graduate school.

During his days and nights in the kitchens of New Orleans, Paul noticed how other workers couldn't read. They struggled just to decipher one-syllable words and abbreviations written out on orders. He tried to help by doing things like writing H-A-M for "hamburger." Every day, Paul said, he would encounter intelligent people who could do a lot of great things, but could not read.

He also met women who spent their lives assembling salads for diners. In a way, said Paul, the city of New Orleans was built on people who did such careful work in the kitchen. But he couldn't stop thinking about what his coworkers might have accomplished with a better education. Looking back, he thought this might have been the time when he decided to stop working in kitchens and go into teaching.

During this same period, he discovered something else about himself: He was very happy being around young children. The epiphany happened when he flew to Iowa to visit his sister's growing family. His two-year-old niece followed him around all day long and chattered, he recalled. She said things that would make him laugh.

The affection was mutual, said Ellen Verret, Paul's cousin. She recalled a rainy summer day when the family gathered for the funeral of an aunt. Around the tomb, people huddled in a half circle under umbrellas. She saw that Paul was standing over to one side, near another grave site, with a nephew.

"It was a tough day and I was looking around. I noticed that Paul had one of the kids. He had taken the little boy and was over at the boundaries of this particular grave. He was allowing the little boy to walk around the boundaries. Paul stayed just behind the boy, letting him walk forward.

"I remember thinking right then how some of us might be inclined to hold the child's hand, some might be inclined to walk right next to him. Paul's style was to walk right behind. It allowed the little boy to look for independence, autonomy. But Paul was also staying where he was needed."

She believed that her cousin opted to teach first grade because he saw it as the make-or-break year for learning to read. But when Paul first walked into Tulane University in the late 1980s to announce that he wanted to be a first-grade teacher, he ran straight into a wall of doubt. Teaching first grade really was not a career choice for thirty-year-old men, he was informed. High school was a more likely option. Maybe middle school.

As Paul saw it, first grade was where the most exciting learning took place, before kids had a chance to grow jaded. "I'll give you an example," he told me. "Last week, one little boy started asking me about where thoughts come from. I said, 'Well, a lot of it comes from what you see and hear, and your senses are giving you ideas as well.' 'But what if you never had'—and this was really kind of a deep question—'all these people talking to you, if you were in a room all by yourself and you didn't see a lot of things, would you still have thoughts?'

"So we started talking about how your brain is wired, and how there are patterns and so forth, and then we started talking about DNA. And this was just one little discussion."

After the DNA lesson, the class then talked about how seeds know which way the root should grow. They talked about how animals are alike but they're also different. They began classifying the objects of nature. When they started moving to another topic, Paul recalled, the boy raised his voice. "Mr. Reynaud," he said. "There's still something I don't understand about DNA."

Moments like those are why he teaches first grade. If children can get one little key to learning, it might open doors. They're less likely to grow up with the worst deprivation of all: to think about life as something that can never be understood.

————

While Paul stayed busy cooking for his and Mary's parents and others at the Tutwiler home, an hour away in Carencro, three households were settling in at Scott and Cindy's house. My newspaper coworker moved out of the house with his dog into a spare room in the house next door. When we realized we weren't leaving anytime soon, my family relocated from Scott and Cindy's living room to four-year-old Evan's room, bumping Evan into his parents' bedroom. We pushed two twin beds together. Some nights our son, Miles, would slip through the crack between the beds. We'd fish him out and go back to sleep.

We found a new routine. While I wrote, Tami searched out pediatric jobs. She called contacts in New Orleans, interviewed in the small towns surrounding Lafayette, and searched national pediatrician job sites. It was difficult to answer our kids' questions about why the old home, their toys, their school, and their friends were so far away. We also knew that we were far more preoccupied than ever before.

Evan was one of Miles's best friends. But the two young boys now stood on shifting turf and were fighting over everything. Miles cried a lot those first weeks. So did we all. But the faces of our children displayed the heartbreaks most nakedly.

Other friends came and went, traveling from city to city on Interstate 10. We finally saw our friend Keith Spera when he passed through one night in mid-September, on his way to a musician's funeral in Texas. Armed with a press pass, he'd been to his family's home in New Orleans East, where his father lived alone for the past several years following Keith's mother's death from cancer.

Keith entered Scott's kitchen cradling a plastic container. Floating in a solution of vinegar and water were the only items he'd taken from the house: his mother's wedding gloves and a lace handkerchief that she had inherited from her mother. He spent the remainder of the night at the sink, gingerly rubbing out tiny flecks of mold. When I awoke the next morning, he was already gone.

On one trip into Lafayette, I stopped at a bookstore to seek out magazine articles about the flood. Paging through an issue of *Time,* I came across a photo of a young boy walking through brown water under outstretched oak branches. He was wearing a green T-shirt with the emblem of the sno-ball stand that was only blocks from our house. The shirt was soaked to the armpits. I recognized him as a boy who played on Cecilia's chess team last year. Walking behind him was his mother. The photo was taken Wednesday, August 31.

At Scott and Cindy's house, the backyard was reserved for delicate conversations. Pecan trees circled the patio, and tiny green geckos hopped from leaf to leaf. On Saturday, September 3, I took the phone outside and called the number I had for Paul Reynaud. At first, I couldn't get through. I dialed again and again.

"Hello?"

"Hello," I said. "Is Paul Reynaud there?"

"This is Paul Reynaud."

The tone was matter-of-fact, the voice from another place and time. I asked how he was doing. "I'm doing great," he said simply.

It took a while for that to register. Then I told him that we were in Carencro and that other families he knew were in nearby towns. I paused. Then I told him that we'd been talking about starting a one-room schoolhouse until we could get back to New Orleans, and I asked him if he wanted to be our teacher.

"That's the best idea I've heard since the hurricane," he said.

Later that day, Tami and I drove to Lafayette to find an insurance office. On the way, she talked on the cell phone with a friend of ours. They were talking about New Orleans. "I can't go back there," I heard Tami say.

I started to shake with anger. Maybe she'd said similar words to me and I didn't choose to hear her. But I knew that the strings that had once held Tami to New Orleans had now snapped. Focused on our day-to-day plans, we barely talked about our future. There was little we could say. By the end of the first week, I learned that my newspaper was planning to reopen. But Tami knew that even if her office opened, there'd likely be no place for her there. She was the most recently hired employee and the only doctor who worked part-time.

All I could think about was New Orleans, and I began to wonder if we'd make it out of this together. It sometimes felt like we woke up one morning and found ourselves rebuilding in different directions. I'd always been the one more enamored with New Orleans; Tami had the stronger emotional ties to our native Midwest. At any rate, we made calls to find Tami a job in New Orleans and came up with nothing.

As we faced painful decisions, the larger tragedy was being calculated. The death toll was rising. Every day we learned new details of how the most vulnerable citizens of the city—old people, poor people, people in hospitals, people in jail—went through the worst of it, with water up to their necks.

One day I reached a friend, Megan Hogard, who taught at a public high school in the Ninth Ward. She had evacuated with her family to Kisatchie National Forest in central Louisiana, planning to make it a weekend camping trip. They had no television and she only learned about the conditions in the city when she started receiving text messages from former students. The kids and their families were trapped in the Superdome. She text-messaged them back to tell them that she had a home in the city's Irish Channel neighborhood, and it hadn't flooded. It was stockpiled with water and food, it was within walking distance from the Superdome, and one window didn't lock.

"They wrote back, 'There's a lot of us,'" she told me. "I didn't care. I wrote back, 'Go.' Then they wrote back, 'They won't let us leave.'"

Megan said that was her breaking point. "I couldn't see

the city the same way," she said. She began planning to move away from New Orleans.

One evening, while biking with Cecilia, I thought I should tell my daughter that there was a chance we might not return to New Orleans to live. I figured that she'd hear us talking about it. I wanted to level with her. So I did. Then I asked her if she had any questions. She didn't.

That evening, as we got ready for bed, I heard Miles start to say, "When I get back to New Orleans . . ." He started to talk about his favorite babysitter, a high school girl named Joy, and how he looked forward to playing with her all day.

"Miles," Cecilia said, "we might not ever live in New Orleans again."

He started crying and I held him. He stopped talking about home.

Each time I drove by the Cajundome in Lafayette, it seemed more impenetrable. I kept hearing from people who tried to enter the Cajundome to help out but were turned away. Then on Labor Day, I finally thought I would have my chance. An event for kids was planned for a park in Lafayette. There would be food and crafts. A volunteer with a local charity told me that children sheltered in the Cajundome would be bused to the park.

Tami and I showed up with our kids at ten in the morning. The temperature was skyrocketing. A Cajun fiddler had set up his band under a tent. He craned his neck and sang out an old tune: *"Tu peux me dire y a un ouragan quand le soleil est bien chaud, mais tu peux pas mettre un macaque sur mon dos."* It translated to: "You can tell me there's a hurricane when the sun is shining bright, but you can't put a monkey on my back." The Hustons arrived, and the kids ran down to the far end of the park for a bicycle race. Then they went under another tent to hear a storyteller.

I looked around but could only see a few children besides our own. I asked about the kids from the Cajundome. They didn't come over, said a volunteer. She told me there were special events planned for them at the Cajundome instead. I later found out that this wasn't true; there were no special events. They just didn't make it to the park. I watched as volunteers pulled wagons filled with boxes of ice cream sandwiches. With few kids around, the sandwiches were quickly melting in the sun.

I passed a table that was stacked with brochures titled "How to Help Child Victims of a Disaster." Inside, it advised not to give any more information than a child is asking for. I thought about how I'd already learned that lesson.

We all arranged to meet with Paul at Mary Tutwiler's house in New Iberia. While I parked the car, the kids ran up the long walkway into the house. A circle of children formed at a kitchen table. At the head of the table was Paul Reynaud.

In front of him, a laptop was open to a Web site with newly available aerial photographs of flooded New Orleans. Paul showed the children how to scan down the streets to see their homes. After a multicourse meal of chicken and brisket that Paul himself had prepared, the children retreated upstairs to an attic, to create a play they would perform later. Their parents sat down with Paul in the library.

Before we could begin talking, another parent of a child at Lusher knocked on the door. He had just returned from New Orleans, where he'd gone to check on his business. He brought with him digital photos of office buildings with corners torn open and computers hanging out the side. He described downed trees, water stagnating on the street, military checkpoints everywhere. We listened in silence. During the first week of September, nothing stopped conversation like a report from home.

Finally, we started talking about the plan that we were then calling "the one-room schoolhouse" or "Willow Street Sanctuary." We asked Paul if he and the kids could come up with a better name. That would be the first day's class assignment, he replied.

Paul said that he'd read an article once about the closing of a one-room schoolhouse in Pilottown, a town on the Mississippi River populated by the families of river pilots who guided big ships through the mouth of the Mississippi. It'd always been his dream to run that kind of school.

We currently had only three families' worth of kids. Paul said he wanted to take in twenty-five or thirty students in all. All of us agreed to help. Finding families would be no problem, we thought. We told Paul we would pay him a salary. Friends around the country had been offering to send money. He simply nodded. He seemed more concerned about when school would start. We didn't have a building. We had no school supplies, no desks. We didn't really know who all might be attending classes. Paul said that no matter what, school should start next Monday, September 12.

Our inaugural parent-teacher meeting finished, Paul led the kids to the Bayou Teche, where they canoed and went fishing with bamboo sticks, using safety pins for hooks and slices of hot dogs as bait. When they returned, we climbed upstairs to see the play that the children had devised. For the most part, it consisted of Eli Poche—a skinny first grader—demonstrating his ability to run around in circles until his pants fell to his knees. Our children were delirious.

Being together counted for a lot, that first week of September. We didn't know who had homes and who didn't; we didn't know who still had jobs. But it was September, and school would begin again. Our school.

CHAPTER 3

On Tuesday, September 6, an e-mail came to my address from Mitzi, one of my daughter's best friends since preschool. It read:

Dere My Friend CeCiLiA
I Have Been Wondering All About You. I thout The Hurricane Killed You? [But I Was Wrong]. I am *So* Glad I Was Wrong. I missed you.

My daughter wrote back:

no I did not die in the Hurricane because I evacuated.

Finding a site for a school proved harder than we'd imagined. A real-estate boom had occurred in southwest Louisiana in the days following Hurricane Katrina. Spare apartments, office spaces, and storefronts were being claimed by evacuees setting up homes and new business locations. In September, Lafayette's *Daily Advertiser* reported, the area experienced a 200 percent increase in home sales over the previous year. In the week following our meeting with Paul, we had driven through a number of prairie towns, peering at houses and shops for a potential classroom, finding nothing.

At the same time, Paul was seeking a home for his parents. It was now being predicted that New Orleans might remain uninhabitable through the winter. His parents had moved from Mary's house to the home of relatives in Lafayette. Now they needed their own place. Paul heard of one available building: an empty office building in the center of New Iberia that most recently had been used by an accountant.

When he walked into the old office, he immediately saw how it could be divided into two sections. His parents could set up an apartment in the front, which had a bathroom and a kitchen; the back was large enough for the school. The building was within walking distance to Mary Tutwiler's house. He could already picture recesses at the Bayou Teche. The town's public library was also a short walk away. Our school had a home.

On Monday, September 12, we drove our kids into downtown New Iberia, past antebellum property near the bayou and into a neighborhood of modest frame houses. We passed a doughnut shop and parked in front of a corner building. A shingle still advertised CPA services. We could feel the pale heat of September as we walked beneath Spanish moss that dripped from oak branches, just as it dripped from trees in the parks in New Orleans. The familiarity was comforting.

Inside, we found Paul in a small room with a large bookshelf. There were a few small chairs—not quite enough for each child—that he had purchased over the weekend. The enrollment was still our neighborhood of three families; we hadn't yet found others to join the school. The children took their seats; that first day, my daughter shared her chair with Olivia Huston.

When he had arrived earlier that morning, Paul realized he didn't have a flag. So he had Cecilia and Olivia color in red and white stripes on a piece of construction paper. Everyone in the class stuck stars onto a blue square. Paul taped it to a yardstick. Then the morning began like school mornings began back home. We stood and recited the Pledge of Allegiance. Paul made some introductory announcements. We attempted to sing a song titled "Each of Us Is a Flower," which Lusher's music teacher used to perform, but we forgot the words.

Looking around at the books, art supplies, and rows of cups ready for dirt and seeds, you could sense the shift. We were now in Paul's classroom. The parents walked outside to a small parking area. We traded information: New Iberia's food-stamp line was supposed to be shorter than the one in Lafayette. We talked about our feelings of panic, about our daily tasks of adjustment and reclamation. We made jokes about the cases of red wine and bottles of prescription pills that now got us through the night.

Willow Street Sanctuary was based on the name of the street that Lusher is located on in New Orleans. A sanctuary is a refuge. This would be our refuge. But a sanctuary is also an asylum. The kids rejected that name.

Instead, on the first day of classes, Paul took suggestions. Some kids came up with names based on their favorite places back home, like Green Market, a Saturday farmers market. Other names sounded like soccer teams, such as The Stars. Hurricane House was another. Then Olivia started talking about the sugarcane fields she'd been looking at every day since the evacuation. The roads to New Iberia from St. Martinville, where the Poches and Hustons now lived, and the path from our new home in Carencro, all cut narrow ribbons through growing stalks of cane. It was our ripening landscape. It was where we landed together. The kids liked the way it sounded.

The vote for Sugarcane Academy was unanimous.

After classes ended Monday, Georgia Flynn was the first parent to arrive. When the others showed up, she asked, "Did you see this yet?" She led us into the former accounting office, which had already been transformed with children's artwork that was rendered in crayon and colored pencil and paint.

As the kids milled about the classroom, nobody eager to leave, Georgia led the way through the main classroom. She pointed out one of the eighteen-by-twenty-four-inch sheets of newsprint that Paul had taped up. It was his daily class note, something I recognized from the previous year. He started each school day by reading through a note, which might address anything from lesson plans to birthdays. Now, Sugarcane Academy's first note included instructions for the school's first project.

Across the top of the page, it read, "WORDS for our hurricane adventure stories." Beside this came a spelling word list: *Hurricane Katrina; house; cars; van; highway; crowded traffic; Lusher School; flooding; levee; gross, dirty, disgusting water.*

Paul had illustrated each word with a line-drawn cartoon, many of them caricatures of himself: a bearded, slightly chubby man, a startled expression on his face, being chased around by the storm.

Georgia pointed to the bottom of the page. There's a story here, the familiar words indicated, and it's just beginning.

"Once upon a time . . . ," it read.

Georgia was a native of Metairie, a suburb to the west of New Orleans. Her husband, Chris Poche, is from Baton Rouge. Like most children in Southwest Louisiana, they grew up accepting hurricanes as a part of life. You certainly never left town because of them. "You'd get your old hurricane tracking chart, my dad would fill up the bathtub with water and he'd buy canned goods," Chris said.

But Georgia and Chris—and their young sons Eli, Adam, and Owen—were now getting used to the routine of the late-summer evacuation. Georgia's college roommate lived with her husband in a roomy St. Martinville home with a big yard and a pool. The kids started calling these trips "evacu-cations."

By nightfall on Saturday, August 27, the Poches and Hustons had all convened in St. Martinville. Georgia's sister, Suzanne, had to be persuaded to leave New Orleans and finally showed up at three in the morning. She had a good reason for not wanting to go. Georgia and Suzanne's mother, Betty Upshaw, remained in New Orleans at Touro Infirmary, where she was in intensive care.

Betty suffered from emphysema and had been in and out of the hospital for the past two years. There was no phone in the Touro intensive care unit. One of the last messages that the Poches had received before evacuating was from a caller who identified herself as Miss Marie. "She said, 'I'm calling for your mother,'" recalled Georgia. "'She said for you guys to leave, that she's fine, and for y'all to make sure you evacuate.'"

So that's what she did. But she struggled with a realization that played on a loop through her mind: She'd left her mom in a hospital; a Category Five was coming to New Orleans; she'd left her mom in a hospital.

She could justify her decision. Hospitals were believed to be the safest buildings in town. They had generators and high floors and trained personnel. Betty's breathing was fragile. A long drive to St. Martinville would have been risky. What if she had an attack on the road, in the middle of nowhere, in a stalled line of traffic?

On Monday, August 29, after Georgia started to hear about

the levee break and flooding in New Orleans, she stayed on the Internet morning and night, searching for news about hospital evacuations. Finally—it was either Tuesday or Wednesday, she later remembered—her mother called. She was at Terrebonne General Medical Center in Houma, about sixty miles southwest of New Orleans. The infants and the ICU patients were among the first to be evacuated from Touro. Betty had slogged with her belongings and her IV pole through the unlit hospital, hearing stories of junkies crashing through the doors searching for drugs, not knowing what to believe.

Now she was in Houma. And before talking about anything else, she wanted to know one thing: Was her son John alive? Georgia's brother lived in Ocean Springs, Mississippi. His wife and children had left to stay with family in Florida. He had decided to ride out the storm.

Those first few days, a chain of doubt linked hundreds of thousands of people across the Gulf Coast, family after family, person after person, with no idea of the fate of someone they loved. The Poches were able to break off their sections of the chain by the end of the week.

At the last minute, John had changed his mind and decided to leave his Mississippi home. Yes, he was out. Yes, he was alive.

Chris picked Betty up at the hospital in Houma. She joined the Poches and Hustons for one memorable night in St. Martinville. At sixty-six, she never lacked for opinions about anything: religion, politics, New Orleans, her children. There was more to say now than ever before. All night, she held court in the kitchen for anyone who would listen. Georgia remembered falling asleep sometime in the early morning, her mother's voice still audible from the other end of the house.

The next day, Betty struggled to breathe. Chris and Suzanne took her to Lafayette General Medical Center and checked her in. The next week, Suzanne drove Betty north to Shreveport, Louisiana, to stay with another son, Steven, and his family. The move made sense. Living in New Orleans, Betty didn't have as many chances to see her Shreveport grandchildren. Plus, there would be less chaos surrounding her the farther she got from New Orleans.

Around this time, the media became absorbed with the question of rebuilding New Orleans. "It looks like a lot of that place could be bulldozed," U.S. House Speaker Dennis Hastert had infamously declared in an interview with an Illinois newspaper after the levees broke. For New Orleanians trying to piece together their lives, such blanket statements sparked panic. Could this become the prevailing wisdom?

In Shreveport, resting in her son's house, Betty picked up her address book and began writing. She filled blank pages and margins with exhaustive lists of names, places, memories. She itemized New Orleans and her life there. She cataloged what she had, what she had lost.

She titled one page, "Home, Ground Zero for me." Under her pen, an arrow pointed to the side of the page, which read

"No other love"; more arrows pointed to the words *childhood, children, grandchildren*. Below that, she wrote, "the air that I breathe."

Down the left side of the page: "Where I learned who I really was and loved it. Where I found gratitude and joy in all my life."

The rest of the page was filled with lines about New Orleans landmarks: the old Zephyr roller coaster at the Pontchartrain Beach Amusement Park, Haydel's Bakery, Popeye's Chicken, Mardi Gras, balconies. Another entry read "long-time friends."

The handwritten list continued on the next page: steamboats, nuns, familiar faces everywhere, her hair salon, City Park, restaurants, the names of all her pets.

The page after that: "amazing graceful city"; "Adam eating Doritos on my bed"; "My beautiful Eli, you taught me how to love again"; "Chris—Tender." About one of her sons, she wrote, "Steven, your daddy's 'button-poppin' joy. The pain broke you, but it made you strong enough to be the most important thing in the world—a loving dad."

She turned the book to the side and drew more arrows: "Let the good times roll! That's the big secret."

Betty would call from Shreveport and joke with Georgia about how her young granddaughter was leading her around the house like she was blind. Then one day, Betty struggled to breathe and became unconscious. Emergency workers arrived and intubated her. They performed CPR. It took sixteen minutes to bring her back. Betty was put on life support; Georgia believed that she had suffered brain damage.

The Poches had scheduled Eli's seventh birthday party in a Lafayette bowling alley. All the Sugarcane kids were looking forward to it. Georgia was determined that this party—this one party—wouldn't be canceled. They hadn't yet told the children about their grandmother. But as the kids bowled and played video games and ate cake, she knew she'd be leaving the next day for Shreveport. She would be saying goodbye. Life support would be turned off. There would be a cremation, like her mother had requested.

Back in St. Martinville, Chris and Georgia told the children that their grandmother had died. That night, Eli went to his father. He told Chris that he wanted to know everything about what had happened to Betty and what would happen to her body.

"By the time Eli and I finished talking, he knew everything I knew about death and dying," Chris said. "He had to know every detail about what was left. He said, 'I know we're 90 percent water, so what's left after cremation? Where do they put her? Can she think right now? When they turn the machines off, will she know anything? Will she know they're doing it? Where will she go?'

"At some point I stopped him and said, 'Eli, you don't have to know this much.' And he said, 'She was my grandmother. I have to know everything.'"

Because funeral homes were understaffed and overbooked in New Orleans, Betty's services at the Garden of Memories cemetery in Metairie couldn't take place until a month after her death.

Eli had always worn shoulder-length hair. He wanted it cut out of respect, he said. He asked Chris if he'd have to be watching as the body was burned. He seemed relieved when Chris explained that the burning had already taken place.

Betty had left specific instructions about her remains. Her first husband, George Flynn, had served in the Air Force and died in combat in Vietnam. Her second husband had died of cancer. She had buried both husbands at the Garden of Memories, in plots next to those of her parents. She had requested that when she died, her ashes be sprinkled over all four grave sites. "I'm the connector," she'd said. Chris and Georgia carried out her wishes. They didn't find out until afterward that sprinkling ashes was against the cemetery's policy.

When it was all over, Georgia didn't think the evacuation had killed her mother. She saw her mother's last words in the address book as a good-bye note from a woman who realized it was her time. Yet in the weeks and months following the hurricane, the obituary pages of the *Times-Picayune* filled with the names and faces of New Orleanians who had died of various causes in cities across the country. Rows of elderly faces looked out from the pages. The city's grandmothers' and grandfathers' last views of their home were of a city underwater.

Among these was Mary Tutwiler's father, Fred Kahn, who was eighty-two and required a breathing machine when he evacuated his New Orleans home with his wife. He spent his last days at his daughter's house, watching through the window as a group of New Orleans children arrived each day at lunchtime and ran screaming down to the bayou. His family cremated his body and had to wait until December to have a memorial service in New Orleans.

His death, Betty's death, the faces in the paper, the deaths of other friends' parents—none of these were counted in the official toll of Hurricane Katrina.

As the children wrote their hurricane stories in their Sugar-cane Academy homework, the school became an oasis. Death had attached itself to us like a shadow. But it never darkened Paul's school.

"We had a good day yesterday," Paul wrote in his class note for Tuesday, the second day of classes. "We planted seeds and we're waiting for them to sprout. Today, we're going to paint portraits. We're going to start learning about sugarcane, too."

He drew a picture of himself next to a towering stalk of sugarcane. Surrounding him were the figures of smiling children.

On another class note, he explained that the students would be painting self-portraits. Portraits, he explained, show what a person looks like. Sometimes they show what a person feels like.

Paul's parents' half of the former accounting office included a kitchen. Cooking became part of the class day. Some of the experiments didn't work out—the children came home one day with wax paper filled with sticky candy that was supposed to be a lollipop. Chocolate-chip omelet day went better. Another new tradition was trips to Meche's Donut King, a local bakery located just a couple doors down from Sugarcane Academy. Every birthday would be celebrated with a doughnut trip.

The first week of Sugarcane Academy, Paul also announced that the school would take its first field trip. "Sugarcane," Paul headlined in his note on the day before the scheduled trip. "Sugarcane is a grass. We use the stem to make sugar. A new plant grows from the roots." On the day of the trip he drew a picture of a car that was headed to "the place where sugarcane grows."

Paul had heard from Mary Tutwiler of the location of a good sugarcane field, across the ditch from a house she used to live in. She led him and the class through the stalks and helped each kid cut down their own cane. She explained the seasonal burning of the sugarcane field, which removes leaves and other unusable parts before the stalks are delivered to the processor. During burning season, New Iberia is ringed by fields of flame and smoke.

When the kids received their own cane, some of the students began marching around. Eli and Walker charged through the field with leaf-topped spears. Returning to the school, they examined the stalks. Like bamboo, sugarcane grows in segments. Each segment has its own eye. And from that eye, new sugarcane grows.

Sitting on the lawn outside the school, Mary and Paul cut open the stalks and gave them to the kids to taste. There were shouts about how horrible it tasted. "The best thing about sugarcane," Mary told them, "is that after you're chewing it for a while, you can spit it on the ground."

Paul listed vocabulary words for cane harvesting and sugar processing: *burned, smashed, ground, cooked, whitened, washed, crystallized*. The kids drew their own sugar-making machines. Some of these were elaborate Rube Goldberg–like devices; others included little hands that came down from the ceiling to perform each step in the production.

The school, like the town of New Iberia itself, shaped itself around the Bayou Teche. The word *teche* comes from the Chitimacha tribe; it translates as "snake." The story goes that a certain poisonous snake, miles long, was an enemy of the Chitimachas. The tribe fought the snake, which, as it died, twisted and turned, carving the path of the bayou.

One afternoon, climbing along the banks of the Teche, the children screamed after discovering a gray, papery snakeskin. The next day, they combed through the snake books at the Iberia Parish Library. They decided that the skin had belonged to a water moccasin.

Mary's backyard became the school's playground and the site of new adventures. When they reached the house every afternoon, the kids would break into a run, past the orange and lemon and persimmon trees. At the bayou, they dug soft holes in the mud among the cypress roots, carefully examining what they found. They pretended to fish.

That first week, four-year-old Callie fell into the water. Her sister, Olivia, jumped in after her. The event would become another school legend. The children would breathlessly replay Olivia's daring rescue and how their teacher just stood there with an annoyed look on his face.

Back at their desks, they continued writing in their hurricane journals. "What do you think New Orleans looks like, sounds like, feels like, and smells like?" Paul had asked at the top of one work sheet. "It sounds like boom, crash, smash," wrote Walker Huston.

For weeks, many of the children believed that the hurricane was still raging in New Orleans. They thought that was why we couldn't return. We didn't learn about this belief until later, after they saw the city for themselves.

My daughter, Cecilia, filled her journal with questions of her own. These questions were more direct than anything she had ever asked me or Tami: "What happened to my town? What does it look like? When can I go back? Does it miss me?"

CHAPTER 4

~~~~~~

The volunteer stared at me from her post at a receiving table at the Cajundome's entrance gate. Silver and green Mardi Gras beads were draped around her neck. She pushed a blank form toward me. "It's been a long day," she muttered. Sitting at the table next to her, a second volunteer looked up quickly and smiled. "Welcome," she said. "You came to the right place."

I told them why I was there: "I'm from New Orleans and I want to spend the night." What I didn't tell them was that I didn't need to stay in the Cajundome. I'd been trying to get into the shelter since the evacuation, and this was my last resort.

In the first week of September, the Cajundome, a 13,000-seat arena that's home to the Ragin' Cajuns college basketball team, became the Lafayette stop on a westward line of sports facilities turned shelters. Stretching from Baton Rouge to Texas, these massive structures boarded tens of thousands of evacuees with nowhere else to go. Some stadiums grew into cities with their own zip codes.

In that first week, I parked my car in the Cajundome lot and walked up to the media table. I showed my Louisiana press pass. Red Cross volunteers shuffled me on to other Red Cross volunteers, but I never could gain entrance.

Others shared my frustration. On the weekend before Sugarcane Academy started, Olivia Huston had told her mom that she wanted to go volunteer at the Cajundome. They drove into Lafayette. But they were turned away. "You're from New Orleans," the volunteer had told them. "You should be resting."

Yet inside was New Orleans—or at least a larger slice of the city than anywhere else in the area. I wondered how families in the Cajundome were doing and how they were dealing with the local schools. I even thought that I might find people who'd want to attend Sugarcane Academy. Paul Reynaud wanted more kids. So did the parents. We had room. We told anyone we could reach to spread the word. A few families seemed interested, but they ultimately moved to another city or put their kids in a local school.

One unfortunate result was that our little school was all-white. The children's school in New Orleans, Lusher, had prided itself on maintaining one of the most racially integrated student populations in the city. That was the kind of school our kids were used to. The first week of classes at Sugarcane, Walker asked how come there were no black kids there. The answer was a difficult one. Many black families we knew from Lusher lived in New Orleans East or Gentilly, two of the most flooded regions of the city. We didn't yet know where they had gone, or if they'd be moving back to New Orleans. We wondered if our old school's hard-won integration was even more fragile than we'd previously thought.

On the evening of Thursday, September 15, I drove once again past the one building in Lafayette that housed more people from New Orleans and the Gulf Coast than any other, and which I knew was largely filled with families who had far fewer options than others. I grew furious at the notion that I wasn't allowed in. Then I realized that I was still a New Orleanian. I could walk in just like anyone else. So I called Tami one evening and told her I was going to check into the Dome. I was spending the night.

It was dusk when I walked up. I read the form that the volunteer had given me. It contained standard questions that all evacuees must answer. Name, address, any phone numbers. The volunteer with the smile then asked me three questions, all medical: "Do you have a cough? Do you have diarrhea? Do you have any open sores?"

Then the first volunteer, who told me she was from Iowa, went to a walkie-talkie and called for a runner to escort me inside. There was silence. The two volunteers talked this out.

"Where are all the volunteers?" asked the Iowan.

"They're dropping like flies," said her partner.

A few more minutes passed. We made small talk, evacuee and volunteers. I had my driver's license to prove my residence, but nobody asked to see it. On the table between us was a spiral notebook, with *Banned and wanted list* handwritten across the cover. The second volunteer explained that the notebook listed the names of residents who broke the shelter rules.

More walkie-talkie. Finally, a lanky volunteer named Skip ambled up. He guided me through a metal detector, asking what I brought with me. Nothing, I said. He took long strides through the concrete corridors that circle the Cajundome. Clusters of cots filled every available space. Cardboard boxes were filled with torn paperbacks and children's toys. Walls were papered with typed or handwritten job offers for everything from mechanics to manicurists. Another announced that a bus of day laborers left every morning to clean up in New Orleans, nine dollars an hour. Other signs stated REPORT ALL CHILD ABUSE TO SHERIFF.

Everyone wore name tags that marked them as either residents or volunteers. Residents' tags included a photo, name, and a New Orleans address. It was possible to read all the addresses, the old streets and neighborhoods, as you walked through the Cajundome. By reading the tags, I noted who lived on Freret Street or Claiborne Avenue, just blocks away from my home in New Orleans. Others lived down the street from where I worked, on Iberville and Banks. We were all jumbled now, like an elaborate puzzle that had been ripped apart.

Skip brought me to Exhibit Hall A, a large room adjacent to the Dome, and went to a side of the room that was lined with metal shelves. He loaded me up on supplies: a long box containing a new metal folding cot; a rolled-up, shrink-wrapped piece of foam; a bundle of sheets, laundered and wrapped in plastic; a Red Cross comfort kit with toiletries; a pillow. Then he steered me to an adjoining room that was marked Exhibit Hall B, chose an empty space near the door, and started setting up the cot.

Next to me, a dirty box spring and mattress sat on the concrete. It was covered with blankets, old stuffed animals, and a brand-new pink Dora the Explorer backpack. On the other side of my cot, an old man squeezed Fixodent onto his dentures. He was from Hollygrove, a neighborhood not far from my house. He was alone; he told me he left when the water in his living room reached a couple feet.

I looked at my cot, which the Red Cross called "sleeping quarters." You would often hear a voice over the loudspeaker that directed evacuees to their sleeping quarters. Skip started to leave, then he frowned at the pillow he'd given me, which was matted and patterned in brown stains. "Sorry about that," he said. Then he shook my hand and was gone.

I sat on my cot and looked around at the rows of cots that stretched out on all sides of me. Exhibit Hall B alone had two hundred cots. Welcome back to New Orleans, I thought.

———

Those first days during the flood, when we started talking about making a school for our kids, thousands of our neighbors were moving either into the Cajundome or through the Cajundome. They came in buses that traveled across Interstate 10 without bathroom stops. They called it a "crazy bus" when nobody in charge seemed to know their destination.

When the Cajundome filled to capacity, volunteers helped evacuees clean up and get food in the parking lot, before sending them west to the Reliant Center in Houston and other shelters. In Austin, Texas, a friend of mine was watching TV when he heard the call for a hundred volunteers to help out at that city's convention center. He assisted people getting off the buses, directing them to cots or triage. He tried to keep families together. He remembered asking one man if he had anybody else with him. The man looked back at him with a blank expression. "They're all gone," the man said.

As a journalist, I visited other shelters in the area. I went to the town of Rayne one Tuesday when I heard that the evacuees there were getting moved out to make room for the annual Rayne Frog Festival. When I showed up, an arena floor was already scrubbed down, and a carnival was setting up on the front lawn, the Ferris wheel taking its first practice spins. Someone told me that the evacuees had all been bused out by nine A.M. the previous Sunday, ahead of schedule.

In a parking lot in Rayne, I found an old woman in a housecoat sitting in front of her daughter's RV. She said that a volunteer had been helping her use the shelter's computer to check on a son who had been in an intensive care unit when the hurricane struck. He was still missing. When the shelter closed, she said, they told her that Rayne's public library had a computer. But she hadn't gone yet.

While on another story about the aftermath of Katrina, I visited a massive gravel lot north of Baton Rouge near the town of Baker. Trailers were beginning to sprout in rows that stretched to the horizon. I met a woman who taught public school in New Orleans. She was with her fifteen-year-old daughter. The woman told me how her daughter had gotten arrested by the police in Baker for fighting. The policeman had said that he knew the New Orleans kids were going to be trouble. Another mother I met said that since the storm, her child was hoarding everything she owned under her bed.

I looked around the gravel lot, which was projected to stay open as an evacuation site for the next eighteen months. People were walking around in circles, trying to distinguish one identical trailer from another. I turned to Tanya Harris, a housing advocate from the organization ACORN, who'd taken me to the park.

"I'm trying to imagine living here for a year and a half," I said.

"So are they," Tanya said.

By the night I arrived at the Cajundome, it housed 2,202 evacuees, according to the *Daily Dome,* a pink sheet of announcements that I saw posted around the arena. There were cots in the Dome, in the exhibit halls, in the back hallways, in the TV room. Some were single cots; others were pushed together and surrounded by a family's entire belongings, like small homes without walls. The air smelled of hand sanitizer. There was no privacy. Everybody saw everybody else sleep, read, take medicine, play cards, braid hair, laugh, cry, or do nothing at all.

Taped-up signs pointed the way to various rooms or hallways for Narcotics Anonymous meetings, housing seminars, jobs, haircuts, meals, showers, prayer. There were reminders everywhere that this new city was squatting in a building that was designed for other uses. My cot was in an area marked CONCESSIONS. A few tables were set up for medical help and counseling around a sign that announced PREMIUM COCKTAILS.

Outside, between the exhibit halls and the Dome, sat a little concrete park. People wandered out there to smoke. Basketball hoops were set up in an area cordoned off by barricades. Two Lafayette policemen watched as young men sank long shots. After only a few hours in the Cajundome, I already had to remind myself that the shelter wasn't a prison. Once you were checked in, you were free to come and go. But you lived amid cots and concrete, surrounded by local police and armed military guards. You were stopped if you weren't wearing a name tag.

A Christian rock show got under way at one end of the park. I walked over to the basketball game, next to the barricades.

There, an old man with long gray hair sat in a wheelchair. I watched him lean over and push a small red fire truck. It rolled across the concrete to a tiny girl who seemed to be about three years old. She pushed the truck back to him. He pushed it back to her. They went back and forth like this for several minutes. On a nearby bench, a woman watched. I guessed that she was the girl's mother.

"See you later," said the man, who wheeled up a concrete ramp into the Cajundome and was gone. The young girl crawled over and sat at the woman's feet. Her face twisted up and she began to cry. It was a miserable, unspecific cry. A passing teenager absentmindedly kicked the fire truck. It bounced away with a clatter. The girl was crying too hard to notice.

I got up to retrieve the fire truck. I pushed it over to the girl and it gently bounced off her leg. She looked up and pushed it back. She drew me into the game. I sat down on the concrete. Then another girl sat down between us. We made a small triangle with our legs and kept the truck in play. A boy sat down beside me. He wanted in. He looked older than the others, and I asked him if he lived in New Orleans. He did. Then I asked him where he went to school. "ISL," he said.

ISL, or the International School of Louisiana, was a small charter school in Mid-City that offered immersion classes in French and Spanish. I knew the school well; we almost sent Cecilia there. We had good friends with kids at the school, friends who almost certainly knew this boy and his family.

After a while, the game ran its course. The little girl

climbed onto her mother's lap. The boy led me to his grandmother, and then his mom. She told me that her family's sleeping quarters were in the center of the main floor, directly beneath the JumboTron. Later that evening, I found them there. While the JumboTron screened the movie *Ray,* we sat quietly together, and she told me her storm story. She told me how this year, like past years, they all went to a downtown hotel, near the Superdome, where her mother worked in housekeeping. The waters rose and they survived, thanks to the manager of a nearby Walgreens who opened up his store for food and supplies.

At one point, she saw two elderly women walking with little purpose through the flood. When she left the hotel to board a bus out of the city, she brought the two women with her. "You probably saved their lives," I said. She nodded.

We talked about schools. She wanted to keep her son's language studies going, so she didn't accept the first school that local administrators offered. She insisted on a school with a French program. I told her about Sugarcane Academy and the teacher who was leading the class. She knew about Lusher. We traded cell phone numbers. She seemed glad to have another option, but I knew she was holding out for a French program. She said that family members were trying to persuade her to go to Atlanta. She didn't feel like moving yet.

It was nearing lights-out. She turned to her kids, readying them for sleep. "I feel at home here," she said.

————

I talked with a few more families that night and told them about Sugarcane. I realized that I must have seemed like an unlikely school recruiter. Before the voice on the loudspeaker directed me back to my sleeping quarters, I wrote a note about the school on a piece of paper and taped it up alongside the other notes. Nobody called.

One woman told me that she'd heard about a school that was up and running inside the Cajundome itself. She didn't have any more details. I walked around, read the signs on the walls, and questioned Red Cross volunteers. If such a school existed, I couldn't find it.

At ten minutes to lights-out, I made my way to Exhibit Hall B. Inches from my cot, the nearest mattress—the one with the Dora the Explorer backpack—was now filled with its occupants. Kids were buried under the blanket, sleeping. Adults talked in low tones. I sat down, picked up my plastic-wrapped package of sheets, and untied the twine. I lifted up a plain white sheet. In the middle were two circular eyeholes. This sheet had once been a ghost.

The lights dimmed. A woman's voice came over the loudspeaker, reading Psalm 89: "Thou dost rule the raging of the sea; when its waves rise, thou stillest them."

After she finished, the exhibit hall fell into a lullaby of coughing, babies crying, old people breathing. People walked out for a smoke, opening and shutting the door with a hollow, metallic click. They brushed past my cot on their way out. Their shadows draped across me as they passed.

I had planned to stay the next day to try to learn if there really were classes being held in the Cajundome. Then I walked outside and saw children sitting in rows, waiting for buses to transport them to area schools. Out in the sunlight, I realized it was a Friday. If I left now, I would be back at Scott Jordan's home in time to drive the kids to New Iberia and Sugarcane Academy. I took off my name tag and walked across the parking lot to my car.

CHAPTER 5

Tami once told me about a musician she saw in the halls of Tulane Hospital in New Orleans. He wore wire-rim glasses and a thin beard and mustache, and carried an accordion and guitar into young patients' rooms. He went by the name Papillion, derived from the French word for "butterfly." When she asked around, she found out that he was a Cajun musician and he played songs for hospitalized kids on his own time.

I reached Papillion after the evacuation and learned that he lived in a town not far from Carencro. He'd been visiting shelters and homes to perform for children who were displaced. He told me he tried to get into the Cajundome, but he couldn't gain admittance through the maze of volunteers. But he found open doors at other, smaller shelters.

At first, Papillion wasn't sure how much he should play the music from home. It might be too painful for kids to hear New Orleans music, he thought. Then, in the town of Opelousas, he was asked by a young boy if he knew the song "Mardi Gras Mambo." The 1954 tune by the Hawketts was a parade anthem—kids in New Orleans grow up with the opening lines the way children in other cities grow up singing "Happy Birthday" or "Jingle Bells": "Down in New Orleans / where the blues was born / it takes a cool cat / to blow a horn." At first, Papillion hesitated. Then a man who identified himself as a pastor from a Ninth Ward church instructed him to play the song. "These children need to be reminded of where they come from," the man said.

I told Papillion about Sugarcane Academy and he offered to drive out to the school. When he arrived, he opened his trunk and pulled out bags of tambourines, drums, triangles, and zydeco rubboards. Inside one of the empty rooms in the former accounting office, the kids formed a small parade around him. Then he started to sing "Mardi Gras Mambo."

Eli Poche interrupted. "Down in Yucky-town," he said.

Papillion stopped the song. "It is dirty there now, but they're cleaning it up," he said. He played some more music and then stopped again. "Did you hear about the zoo?" he asked. "How the animals are okay?"

"All the fish in the aquarium died," Eli said.

"That's true," said Papillion. "A lot of them did." He played some more. "But people all over the world are going to help."

"I have a fish," said another student, "and it didn't die."

"A lot of good things happened," Papillion said. "A lot of people have learned to be kinder."

"I'm going back to New Orleans," Olivia Huston announced.

The class launched into more talk about the city they hadn't yet seen since the hurricane. Papillion started an old song by the Meters, another local classic for kids. "I went on down to the Audubon Zoo," he sang, "and they all ask'd for you." The children picked up the tambourines. The youngest ones marched around in a circle. Papillion sang another round of New Orleans tunes.

Throughout September, the student population at Sugarcane Academy hovered at around a dozen students. A few kids came and went. Cecilia's second-grade teacher at Lusher, Megan Neelis, moved to New Iberia with her husband and young children: Christine, a kindergartner, and Harry, who was in preschool. Megan began running a preschool in an empty room in the former accounting office. Ever since Callie fell in the bayou, Paul seemed eager to put someone else in charge of the youngest kids. Henry Reynaud, a first grader and Paul's nephew, also joined the school. So did Rex Collins, a first grader, and his sister Abby, a preschooler.

Rex and Abby's father, Rich Collins, was an old friend and former coworker at *Gambit*. A few years back, he helped launch the Imagination Movers, a band that performs children's music. Our kids were fans; so were many others in

New Orleans. Following the hurricane, parents and children wrote to the band's Web site to see how the musicians fared. One e-mail read, "On Tuesday when the water started rising, Caroline turned to me and her first question was, 'Mom, do you think the Movers are OK?'"

The Movers were okay, but barely. The band lost its instruments and equipment. Three members saw their homes flood, including Rich and his wife, Becky. One band member, Scott "Smitty" Smith, was a firefighter who stayed in New Orleans during the flood to help conduct searches for survivors. After the flood, Smitty wrote "We Got Each Other (The Evacuation Song)," with a reggae beat and the lyrics, "We got each other to lean on. / Wherever we end up, we'll call it home." They posted the song on their Web site. We downloaded it and put it on a CD. It played in our car as we drove to New Iberia each day.

Rich said that when they evacuated, he and Becky told their children that they could each bring just one toy. Rex couldn't decide which stuffed animals to save and which ones to leave behind. "When we left, we left in a hurry," Rich recalled. "He was brokenhearted." As Rex's parents loaded the van, his family quickly worked out another solution: Rex placed his four favorite stuffed animals on a plastic bin in his room and covered them with a large sombrero for protection.

Their house, in the Mid-City neighborhood near City Park, stewed in deep water. When Rich and Becky could return, they pushed open the front door, which was blocked by a player piano that had landed on its side. At first, only some family silver was salvageable from the pasty muck. Then Rich climbed over more furniture to get into Rex's room. There, he saw the plastic bin, still upright. Rich figured it must have floated up with the tide and then settled back down, with the sombrero keeping the animals clean. When he told me the story, he laughed at how ridiculous it must have sounded. But with every family photo gone, every heirloom destroyed, the survival of stuffed animals seemed crucial. They now had a story to tell about how Rex had saved a sombrero's worth of animals.

By the end of September, the Collins family found an apartment near New Orleans, where Rich could help put the band back together. Around the time that the kids said good-bye to Rex and Abby, we got a call from another family. Jerry Schumacher was a high school history teacher in New Orleans. He and his family were now staying with his brother in Carencro, bedding down in a trailer in the backyard with their four children, whose ages ranged from first grade through high school. Jerry had found work at Lafayette High School. He was being paid as a substitute, without benefits or health insurance. In late September, they learned that Jerry's wife, Linda, was expecting their fifth child.

The Schumachers had enrolled their oldest children in high school in Lafayette, and their two youngest children—Hannah and Culloden—at a rural elementary school. But at the country school, the rules were strict, Hannah reported back to her parents. You had to walk down the halls with your hands behind your back. There was no talking during lunch. She was miserable. The family found their way to Sugarcane Academy.

We began carpooling with the Schumachers, meeting early in the morning at a gas station off the highway. We'd drive the hour to school and play our Imagination Movers CD on the way. Cecilia began going over to Hannah's trailer. They'd run in the grassy fields and climb up to a tree house. They found tiny clams in a stream and gave each one a name.

Fall was settling over southwest Louisiana. Scott Jordan put out the Halloween decorations. Miles and Evan each got new bikes with training wheels. It was disconcerting to see a season change around us when we still felt stuck in time. Yet New Orleans was opening up. Friends would call me nearly every day to say they were going in, or that they'd just been in. There were passes and forms and documents that you could usually just wave at a checkpoint.

I didn't want to go yet. I had a good sense of what I'd see: soldiers armed with M16s, military bases on our old playgrounds. Trees eviscerated, wintry. Quiet neighborhoods punctuated by burned houses, felled oak trees, tableaus of destruction. Friends described it as an abandoned movie set; they called it apocalyptic. I didn't want to see our block, silent as a graveyard, which in New Orleans is called a city of the dead because it is built above the ground.

———

Paul Reynaud launched into his lecture about Halloween the way he began most lectures: the Socratic way, with questions. "Why do we give away free stuff for trick-or-treating?" he asked. "Why do we give away candy?"

He sat in a metal folding chair. The dozen kids sat on the floor around him. Hannah spoke up first. "Uh, maybe they don't want it?" she asked.

"They don't want it," Paul repeated. "They don't want candy? Hmm . . ."

"People don't *need* candy," said Walker.

"Yeah, some people are like Mr. Reynaud," said Eli. Paul Reynaud was notorious among the kids for not liking sweets.

"You'll give away a lot of candy because you don't like it," Walker said.

"We'll see," Paul said. "Now, think back. Because Halloween has been around for not just a hundred years, or the last fifty years. It's been around for thousands of years. Anthropologists say it goes way, way back, when *peopllle* . . . didn't even live in cities."

Whenever he spoke to his students, he elongated words like *people,* as if slowing down his stride to let the class catch up. He was in no hurry; a class discussion might circle around a topic for quite a while. Especially today. The preschool had joined the conversation.

He continued: "Before people lived in towns and cities and places like that, when people lived out in the country or when people lived out in farms all by themselves . . ."

"Was it when cavemen were alive?" asked Christine Neelis.

"No, I wouldn't say quite as far back as cavemen, but not too much more recently than cavemen. Miles, yes?"

"Why are we talking about Halloween stuff?" Miles asked.

"Because we are studying about Halloween."

"Maybe it's before George Washington died," said Olivia.

"No, it's a lot before," said Paul. "George Washington lived about three hundred years ago; this is more like thousands of years ago."

"Oh."

Paul picked up the thread again. "Okay, think about this: If you lived out in the country, a lot of people used to farm back then. And if you had things that you grew, this would be the time that you would cut it down and harvest it.

"Remember that people didn't have electricity, there were no lights outside. So it was very dark out there, and it started getting colder, the days started getting shorter. And their fields would be empty, and they'd store everything in their barns. And you went out there and it gave you an eerie feeling. Because where things had been growing all spring and all summer long, suddenly, it was all cut down.

"You'd go by a cane field. Imagine if everything looked like those cane fields, where all the cane was cut down. See little stumps down there in the ground, but everything else was gone. It looks kind of . . . scary.

"And some people used to think, this is what some anthropologists say, people thought that when all the plants were cut down then, that was the time when the spirits could rise out of the ground. The ground was going to be full of spirits."

"Dead people," said Olivia.

"Not just dead people, but also spirits that lived down there. Things like goblins . . ."

The class began shouting examples. "Dinosaurs!"

"Not so much dinosaurs—people didn't really . . ."

"Vampires!"

"Batman!"

Paul paused. "People thought there were spirits, not always evil spirits, that lived in the earth," he continued. "And when you cut all that stuff down, they could rise up. Now, you were supposed to light a fire and the fire was supposed to scare the spirits away. And so there are some places where people would light fires. But if you light a fire out in the open, it might catch the other crops on fire. What they would do is they would put these fires inside something. Like a . . . *holllowed-out* . . ."

"Pumpkin!"

"Like a pumpkin, or a gourd. Pumpkins actually came from America, so pumpkins didn't even come into this thing until about two hundred, three hundred years ago. But before that . . ."

"A monster!"

". . . people would hollow things out, and they were supposed to scare the evil spirits. And on this night, they said evil spirits would wander from door to door. You had to have something to give them so they wouldn't try to come into your house. And that's where we get our idea of . . ."

"Trick-or-treating!"

"Trick-or-treating. But why do you dress up in costumes?"

"To be like the evil spirits!"

"You're supposed to be like the evil spirits. It's sort of like commemorating what people used to think a long time ago."

"And some people leave the candy outside," Olivia said. "Maybe they do that so spirits won't want to come inside their house."

"I don't think that people nowadays really think about it very much. Actually, now, it's kind of funny, because a lot of churches don't like Halloween very much. They have harvest festivals and do other kinds of things. But in the Catholic Church, the day after Halloween is called All Saints' Day. And it's supposed to be the day we honor all the saints, all the dead people. It kind of goes with Halloween, too."

Eli scowled. "The Saints aren't dead," he said. "They're a football team."

After watching Paul deliver his Halloween lecture, I stayed after school to ask him about his teaching method. He talked about the idea of integrated learning, in which the various subjects—math, science, literature, art—are recognized as being interconnected. But he didn't seem to want to put a label on what he does in the classroom.

In recent years, he said, he'd noticed how schools use coordinators to drop into classrooms to make sure that teachers are keeping lesson plans on track. Teachers must follow a script that sometimes leaves little room for improvisation. "You had this feeling that you were supposed to back off on riffing," Paul said. "But if lessons were going really well, you'd want to let them keep playing."

A classroom is shared between the teacher and students, he said, and teachers need to listen to students instead of just lecturing to them. "For a teacher, it kind of opens you up to hearing, 'We're bored' or 'We don't like this.' And once you open up that dialogue, it's hard to shove it back in a box."

The main thing that he'd learned so far at Sugarcane Academy, he said, was that school didn't depend on books, or on having the right colored marker. "In the first couple weeks, it was just like, 'Okay, I'm going to talk to you for a little while, and then I want you to write something for me.' It was really a pure form of teaching."

By the middle of October, I learned that Paul Reynaud and his parents were ready to go back home. So were most Sugarcane Academy families. One afternoon after school, as the children played in their classroom, their parents sat on the floor in an adjoining room. We took turns saying whether we wanted to return to New Orleans. Most did. So we came to an agreement: We'd end classes in New Iberia on Friday,

October 28. We would resume the school somewhere in New Orleans on Monday, November 7.

We didn't know where in New Orleans we'd hold the school, or how big it might become. But we'd been hearing from people who were returning to the city and were looking for a place to send their children. Like we did in New Iberia, we set an opening date even when we didn't have much else. We decided that we'd hold Sugarcane Academy– New Orleans through the rest of the calendar year, expecting that local schools would open their doors in January.

After the meeting, Kiki Huston and I walked out of the school together. She knew that I was hoping to stay longer in New Iberia. "I was worried you'd be upset," she said. I thought about how to answer her. "It's time to go back," I said.

I wasn't sure how to reintroduce the children to New Orleans. Then on Saturday, October 15, I heard of an event for evacuees called Fun Day, which would take place in a park in Baton Rouge. Nickelodeon and Rosie O'Donnell were sponsors, and the Imagination Movers would even perform. For the first time since the storm, I drove the kids west on Interstate 10. Baton Rouge was about halfway between Lafayette and New Orleans.

About five thousand people showed up for Fun Day, including some of our friends from New Orleans. All around us, children jumped inside inflatable castles and dragons while parents talked about their plans. Then, around midafternoon, without planning it and without being sure if our house had water or electricity, I asked Cecilia and Miles if they wanted to keep driving east, to New Orleans. They screamed at me as if I'd just offered to drive them to Disney World.

We were going home. That weekend, Tami was in Chicago, interviewing for a job. I couldn't even think about that possibility. I just had to keep moving. Keeping the kids nearby helped.

After their day in the hot sun, they fell asleep in the backseat. I waited until we crossed Lake Pontchartrain to announce our arrival. "We're in New Orleans," I called out. They peered out the window. Except for a few mangled billboards and a large self-storage unit with its sides blown out, the view from the interstate looked fairly normal. I asked the kids where they wanted to go.

"I want to see the old house!" Cecilia shouted.

"The old house!" Miles repeated.

There were no checkpoints anymore; we drove easily into the Broadmoor neighborhood, where we'd lived only two years earlier. The children started to recognize the streets, even though there were no standing street signs. Old refrigerators, strapped shut, lined the sidewalks. Cecilia read aloud the epithets that had been spray-painted across the refrigerator doors. They cursed the president, or FEMA, or they bore whimsical slogans like DO NOT OPEN UNTIL HALLOWEEN.

Surrounding the refrigerators were mounds of box fans, beds, bathtubs, toilets, chairs, and toys. The kids' attention was drawn to the stuffed animals and dolls that poked their heads out of the debris. "It's not fair," said Cecilia whenever she passed a toy that had been shoveled to the street.

We drove around and visited our personal landmarks: Treadway Pediatrics; Memorial Medical Center, where Tami had seen her last baby before evacuating on Sunday, and where doctors and patients had been stranded for days during the flood; Ted's Frostop, a root-beer stand where a giant mug sign toppled off its pedestal and now lay upside down on the sidewalk. Boats that had transported our neighbors during the flood now were beached on the sidewalks.

Miles looked out the window. "All the things in New Orleans are so crazy," he said.

I turned down Rocheblave Street and slowed down in front of our old house. The water—*water* being a euphemism for the mixture of Lake Pontchartrain and sewage that covered most of the city—had risen past the porch and left its brown stain halfway up the front door. Next door, our neighbors had already turned their house inside out. Everything we remembered from parties at their house—the couch, the piano, chairs—was on the sidewalk. We drove on without stopping.

We parked in front of our own house. As I suspected, it hadn't flooded. When I walked inside, I tried the electricity. It worked. It was a painfully familiar feeling, walking through the doorway. Inside, it looked like a shrine to late August. The Sunday *Times-Picayune,* with the KATRINA TAKES AIM headline, still lay on the couch where Tami had left it when she loaded the cats into the car and drove off. Homework from the first week of school lay on the kitchen counter.

Bill Parsons—the neighbor who had helped us size our plywood for Hurricane Ivan just one year earlier—was in the neighborhood with his family. His daughters were staying in Alabama but were home for the weekend. They saw us drive by and ran down the street and into our open front door. Little hands pulled down our kids' toys. The house sputtered back to life.

Down the street, Paul Reynaud's car was parked—once again—in front of his classroom. While the kids played in the near-empty neighborhood, I walked down to see him. He was mopping up the water that had seeped into his first-floor classroom. He was still dressed in the same button-down clothes he wore each day to school, but now sweat poured down his face as he hauled books and chairs to the street.

The children all slept with me that night. The city was dark and quiet. As I listened to them breathe, I wondered just what they had been seeing, what they had been thinking. I wondered how I could teach them anything about what had happened to their city.

The next morning, I found a box of cereal bars in the cupboard. I washed their hands with water from silver cans labeled DRINKING WATER that we had obtained at a Lafayette food-donation center. Then I decided that I would take a cue from what I'd learned at Sugarcane Academy: No matter how I might be feeling, I'd do my best to make this an adventure for Cecilia and Miles.

At the Fun Day in Baton Rouge, actors from the TV show *Blue's Clues* had passed out spiral-bound *Blue's Clues* notebooks and pencils. I handed the notebooks to the children and announced that we were going to explore our neighborhood. I told them how people had been helping to make sure our neighbors were safe: They had painted on the houses to show that all the people and animals were all right. The kids had already seen the mark—the painted red X.

The Katrina search-and-rescue signs varied in appearance throughout New Orleans. In our neighborhood, the top quarter of each X revealed the date of visitation. Most indicated early September. The left side bore the name of the National Guard unit or other search-and-rescue team. The right usually indicated if there were animals in the house. The presence of human bodies was indicated in the bottom quadrant.

When we drove through our neighborhood on the previous evening, I had checked for *D.B.* in the bottom quadrant of the Xs, or any other markings that might indicate *dead body*. If they were there, I didn't want the kids to see them. But there was nothing like that in the blocks around our house.

As we set out down the street, I told the kids that these markings showed that everyone was safe. I didn't tell them

that other markings around the city indicated the opposite—
that some people weren't safe. Looking back, I wonder if they
figured that out themselves.

We turned up Plum Street. We couldn't walk on the sidewalks; nails stuck out of plywood, and power lines hung like
strands of spaghetti from low tree branches. Swarms of flies
were everywhere. With no cars in sight, I took the kids down
the center of the street. There, Cecilia found an old spray can
that had been left behind by a search-and-rescue team. She
made her own *X* on the pavement.

We walked the block up to the Hustons' house. Kiki was
there this weekend to clean up. The Hustons had left their
cats behind and, a few days after the storm, had found someone in New Orleans to break a window and shove dry cat
food into the house. Kiki had come to the city to clean up the
glass and haul out the furniture that the cats had destroyed.
Her front door was open. As we approached, I could hear her
on the phone with her mother.

"Because it's our home," she said.

There was silence. "I know it might happen again," Kiki
said. "In fact, I know it will happen again."

We turned back without talking to her. On the way to
our house, we passed another open door. It led to an apartment where Joaquin lived. The five-year-old had moved here
with his parents within the past year from Venezuela. He and
Miles had immediately become friends; they used to sing along

to a They Might Be Giants song about the letters *Q* and *U,* with their arms around each other.

"Hey Joaquin!" I shouted at the open door, but I immediately regretted it. A strange woman came out to the front porch. I looked past her and saw that the rooms were empty. She told us that Joaquin and his parents had moved out. They were here just the other day and had packed up a truck and left.

We returned to the middle of the street to walk home. Miles fell quiet. "This hurricane is long," Cecilia said.

On our drive out of New Orleans, I turned from the interstate onto the West End exit. A friend had told me that FEMA was beginning to erect a trailer park on a wide swath of land by a canal. The only person I could find was an ABC cameraman. He hadn't heard about a trailer park.

When I tried to make a turn to go back to the interstate, all the roads were closed. Without intending it, I was driving my children deeper into Lakeview, closer to the 17th Street Canal breach. Some of these houses looked like freight trains had pummeled through their brick walls. In this neighborhood, I couldn't predict what markings Cecilia might be able to read.

I turned onto Fleur de Lis Drive and we passed cars that were covered in ash. There was a sour smell in the air and dust was blowing into the car. I could taste it on my lips. I closed the vents and the inside of the car heated up. Our few minutes in Lakeview seemed like an eternity. With nothing to do but drive through it, I turned up the music and drove as quickly as I could back to the interstate.

On the way back to Carencro, I turned off the CD player and asked the kids about what they'd seen in New Orleans. I asked them if they had any questions.

"Why didn't we evacuate a long time ago?" Cecilia asked.

"What do you mean?"

"Mommy said that we knew a hurricane would come. So why didn't we evacuate before?"

"Well, what do you think?"

"Because our friends are here." Then she added, "I'm not going to move away. And if I move away, I'm not going to make new friends."

I realized that she must have heard our ongoing discussions about moving. We had talked in the car when we thought they were listening to the music; we had talked in the bedroom when we thought they were asleep. I couldn't dispute the fact that Tami had lost her job and needed to find another one. But this was no way to leave your home. We discussed the possibility of Tami leaving for Chicago early, with me staying behind with the kids. But I silently wondered how, once we separated, we would find our way back together.

I had no answers for Cecilia. I didn't even try.

———

Friday, October 28, the last day of school in New Iberia: It began, like all days, with a morning meeting. The kids gathered on the floor, dressed like royalty and superheroes and monsters for an afternoon Halloween party. Paul Reynaud announced first that it was Christine Neelis's birthday.

Christine raised her hand. "Doughnuts," she said. The students launched into more discussion about this. "Oh wait, we have talking during morning meeting?" Paul interrupted. The students quieted. Doughnuts might be in jeopardy. "Today we have regular morning work," he continued. "We're going to have regular reading, we're going to have regular writing, we'll slip in math, which is, of course, very important. And we're going to walk over to the bayou one last time today, and we're going to have lunch there."

The kids cheered. A new student, Carter, had even brought real fishing poles.

"We're going to have lunch in the backyard, and we're bringing bird feeders to put on the deck. What else?"

"Sounds pretty much like a normal day," Walker said.

"Yeah, pretty much like a normal day," Paul said. "And then we'll come back here and do a science project. And that's pretty much it."

"What about the Halloween party?" Harry Neelis asked. Paul acted as if he hadn't noticed that the kids were in costume. "Oh yeah, right," he said. "We're planning on having a Halloween party but it's only if we finish up all of our regular work, because we have regular work, too. Now, if you're wearing a costume that involves a hat or googly eyes or a nose or something like that, it's probably a good idea to leave it in your cubby because it's . . ."

"Distracting!" the kids shouted.

"It's distracting. Thank you very much. If you've learned one word here . . . Harry?"

"On Christine's birthday, we got string, and Meche's doughnuts."

"We usually have doughnuts," Christine said. "We have string. You put a doughnut on the end, and then you try to eat it without any hands."

Paul considered it. "Sounds like a great idea," he said.

Next came the morning song. Chris Poche brought in a guitar, and Derek Huston had his saxophone around his neck. Someone phoned Mark Hughes, Lusher's music teacher, so he could listen in. "One, two, three—Good morning, Mr. Hughes!" the kids shouted into the cell phone. Then Chris and Derek started playing a medley of songs, ending with "When the Saints Go Marching In." They changed the lyrics to "When the Monster Bites Off Your Head."

When it was over, Paul promised that if the kids put away their hurricane journals quietly, they'd all go to Meche's for doughnuts. There was another cheer.

"Today rules!" Walker shouted.

The parents arrived for the Halloween party to paint the children's faces, supervise games of ghost bingo, and help make spider crowns out of black construction paper. I stood inside the old accounting office and looked around at the art-decorated walls and the shelves filled with books and games. It was all about to change again. Our oasis was being packed up and carted down the road.

I asked the kids what they liked most about Sugarcane Academy. They recalled the field trips around the area. On a tour of the Tabasco factory, they took turns daring each other to put hot sauce on their tongues. As they walked on the grounds, a bobcat crossed their path. When they visited Acadian Village, a historic re-creation of a Cajun community, they sat at the wooden desks of an actual one-room schoolhouse.

I asked Walker Huston what he liked best. Usually when Walker talked to me, he went for a laugh. This time, he gave me a serious answer. "Because it's so beautiful," he said. "And because Mr. Reynaud's here."

In a room down the hall, Tami was wrapping kids in toilet paper, turning them into mummies. Their eyes barely visible, the children walked around with hands outstretched, bumping into one another. With the kids gone from the main classroom, I picked up the oversized notebook—the one that Paul posted in the class to describe lessons and activities—and paged through the days.

"Today is my second first day of school this year!" he'd written on September 12. "I'm a little scared. I hope the kids aren't too mean to me." Beneath those words, he had drawn a cartoon of himself reading a book that was titled *How to Be Mean*.

Another page listed the possible names for the school. One after that listed the ways that New Iberia and New Orleans were different and the ways in which they were the same. In New Iberia, Paul had written, "Normally less people, now more people." In New Orleans, he'd written, "Normally more people, now no people." He underlined the word "no" twice.

Olivia Huston walked into the room. She sat down and began looking through the pages with me. "I'm going to miss it," she said about the New Iberia school. "But we've been gone for, like, eight weeks." Culloden and Hannah followed her. "The other school felt strange," Culloden said about the rural school he'd started right after evacuating. "Sometimes when I had recess, I didn't have anyone to play with."

They told me about Elizabeth Kahn, who used to be the school librarian at Lusher Elementary, and who also evacuated to New Iberia. She began checking out books at the Iberia Parish Library and leading storytime with the kids. Then we paged through some more class notes. On one day, the children chose poems to act out. On another, they learned about different types of sugar.

We arrived at the page for the day that the children learned that the bayou parade for New Iberia's Sugar Cane Festival was canceled; Hurricane Rita was in the Gulf. The storm hit the border of Texas and Louisiana on Saturday, September 24, devastating towns along the coast. The Ninth Ward in New Orleans flooded again; evacuees from Rita joined evacuees from Katrina in the shelters. Yet even when the local schools announced closings, Paul said we would meet at Sugarcane Academy. For a time, it looked like we might be the only school operating that day in southwestern Louisiana. Finally, on Friday, Paul called us to say he had to help board up windows and was reluctantly calling off classes.

As the kids and I kept paging through the class notes, other parents were removing the art from the paneled walls and piling up the landscapes, self-portraits, and pictures of sugar-making machines. By dinnertime, the old office building looked exactly as it did two months earlier, before we ever moved a school into its rooms.

CHAPTER 6

On Halloween night, the Schumachers joined us in Carencro for trick-or-treating. Hannah and Cecilia dressed as witches and went running from house to house, their pointed hats flopping. Then, as we joined other families at a party in Scott Jordan's neighborhood, Cecilia turned to me. "We're moving! I don't want to move!" she said loudly and without warning. I stop and kneeled in the road to face Cecilia. She didn't want to talk anymore about it.

We didn't resume the conversation until the next day, during our first trip out of Louisiana since the storm. We were driving to Houston to fly to Chicago, to visit schools and figure out the other details of our move. The new plan was to stay in New Orleans through December. When Sugarcane Academy closed, we'd go north.

On the way to Houston, I drove alone in the front seat. Cecilia and Miles sat in car seats in the back, with Tami between them. I told Cecilia and Miles that we could maybe finish out the school year in New Orleans. Tami could move to Chicago early and we could join her there in the summer. Cecilia pantomimed her rejection of that timetable. She shook her head from side to side and tightly grabbed Tami's arm. That settled it. We'd leave Louisiana together after Christmas.

The Hustons had already returned to New Orleans by Halloween. On the morning of October 31, Kiki woke up with a feeling of dread; she asked herself just what she was doing with her children in New Orleans. It was an unsettling place. During the day, a few people walked around the neighborhood, taking stock of houses, cleaning up branches, hauling refrigerators to the sidewalk. That afternoon, the children got dressed up in capes and princess dresses. When darkness fell, they all went outside and discovered that they were the only trick-or-treaters around. Houses were still empty. They all walked down the center of deserted streets, fallen tree limbs snagging their costumes. Mark Hughes's house was nearby and was lavishly decorated for the holiday, just like always. The Hustons made their way to their music teacher's home and were showered with candy. They ended the night in the parking lot of Children's Hospital, where Papillion was performing a free concert for kids who'd found their way back to the city.

"I thought it was going to get better from there, and it didn't. It got worse," Kiki said of their first days home. With

Derek working on the road as a musician, she found time to go out on her own to drive through the rest of the city, away from the small slice that hadn't flooded. She made trips into Lakeview and the Ninth Ward. She didn't want to go with anyone else. It was a personal loss, she said, and that's how she had to experience it.

She'd been in love with New Orleans for years, ever since she and Derek first drove down from Washington, D.C., in the early 1990s. They had arrived on a Halloween day and never left. Their first stop had been a neon tavern in the Ninth Ward called the Saturn Bar, where they'd punched in Fats Domino and Ernest Tubbs songs on the jukebox. Derek eventually started playing saxophone with brass bands and then helped launch a popular local band called the Iguanas. They married in City Park, and when they had children, they taught them to love New Orleans as much as they did.

But one night after returning from the evacuation, Walker burst out crying. The city was so messy, he said. Kiki realized that he'd been looking at the flooded buildings when they drove down Freret Street and Claiborne Avenue. His eyes trailed the brown waterlines, just like her eyes did. "The first good rain we had, they all got nervous," she said. "They wondered if another hurricane was coming. And I had to wonder, will they ever feel safe here again?"

Kiki said she considered herself an optimist by nature. She believed that you live your life by focusing on something that's good and then moving toward it. And every time she looked at her cell phone, it announced new messages. Parents had returned to the city and had heard rumors about a school called Sugarcane Academy. Without ever specifically being assigned or volunteering, Kiki took on the job of organizing the growing school. Returning to a devastated New Orleans, this job suited her just fine.

A parents meeting was set for Thursday afternoon, November 3, at a section of Audubon Park near the Mississippi River. A couple dozen parents arrived. Paul Reynaud and Megan Neelis were there, along with Robin Delamatre, another teacher from Lusher. Children saw friends they hadn't seen in two months. New kids quickly joined in. They ran to a nearby playground while parents and teachers talked.

The owners of a possible site for Sugarcane Academy had pulled out just the day before, citing insurance worries. Kiki admitted that she didn't have an alternate building. Someone brought up the idea of splitting up the children into age groups and using people's houses as classrooms. It wouldn't really feel like a school, but it might be the best option. As in New Iberia, Paul Reynaud believed that the important thing was to stick to an opening date. No matter what, school would begin next Monday.

Not everyone felt so sure it would happen. "It was four days before we were supposed to start, and in my heart I thought, 'We don't stand a chance,'" Inta Phayer later said. Originally from Australia, she and her husband, Kevin, had lost their restaurant business in the flood. They returned to

New Orleans to set up a catering company for downtown workers. But their four children had no school—and Inta didn't see how there'd ever be one by next week. People no longer help anyone, she thought, because everyone in this country is so afraid of being sued.

Although a few structures were torn and battered from the storm's high winds, most of the park along the river was relatively untouched by the hurricane. Looking around, you could imagine the New Orleans that had existed just three months earlier. The view offered no comfort to Cathy Franklin as she listened to the other parents discuss a school without a building.

Everyone was sounding so positive that she didn't want to voice her own doubts. But since the weekend of the hurricane, Cathy, an associate professor in the communications department at Loyola University, had been living apart from her husband, Danny. She had evacuated with her two daughters to her parents' house in the central Louisiana city of Alexandria. She was now being discouraged from returning to New Orleans and its uncertainties. Danny was a sergeant in the Louisiana State Police who had stayed on duty in New Orleans throughout the storm. He didn't think the family should move back. At least not yet. It made sense to him that the girls finish out the calendar year in the good schools they had found in Alexandria. Cathy's parents agreed.

The Franklins had nowhere to live in New Orleans. The first floor of their house had flooded. Cathy reminded herself that she had just paid two hundred dollars to put the girls in a drama club in Alexandria. Rehearsals ended with a big Christmas performance. Danny was now being housed with other state troopers in a hotel in LaPlace, near New Orleans. Cathy remembered that her own daddy sometimes had to work away from the family when she was growing up, and that her mother's daddy traveled with his oil job. But this was different, she thought, as she watched her daughters run across the field with friends. They belonged at home in New Orleans, now more than ever.

So when Kiki announced there was no location for Sugarcane Academy, Cathy's heart sank. She thought of her parents, and she thought of Danny. It was going to be a hard sell.

In Alexandria, the nights had been the hardest. On the Saturday before the storm hit, sixth grader Claire Franklin never told her mother that she was using her grandparents' computer to e-mail her father. A little after eight o'clock, she started typing. She began with the subject line "worried." Then she continued:

> daddy is the hurricane goin to hit?
> I hope you will be okay!
> where are you goin to stay when the hurricane hits
> mommy said oshner hospital
> is she right
> I'm really worried about you

I really really really really wish that there was no such thing
as a hurricane
wat if you get hurt
please e-mail me back in a hurry
with much much much much much much much much much
as many muches as you can think of much love, love Claire

Claire clicked *send* and went to sleep. When she woke up
the next morning, the mandatory evacuation was in effect for
New Orleans. The mayor's order didn't include her father.

Cathy, her parents, and her daughters dressed for church.
They attended the Pentecostals of Alexandria, a large church
started in 1950 by evangelist G. A. Mangun and his accordion-
playing wife, Vesta. It was the church of Cathy's childhood, a
place where high emotion was allowed through the doors.
Now, singing along with the band and massive choir, Cathy
could feel hot tears streaming down her face. Casey, her first
grader, asked to be picked up. "No crying, Mama," she said
when she reached eye level.

Cathy tried to keep the girls away from the television that
night. At seven o'clock, Claire received an e-mail back from
Danny. "Thank you for thinking about me," he had written.
"I'm going to be OK. I'm going to be staying at one of the hospitals. I love you, Casey and Mommy very very much! Daddy."

The state closed down the troop headquarters Sunday
night. Some troopers went to Baton Rouge. With about

twenty others, Danny bunked down at the police department in Kenner, a New Orleans suburb. When the storm hit Monday morning, he could see the ceiling tiles shake. Rain blew across the window in horizontal lines. Across the street from the police department, a restaurant slowly disintegrated in the wind. Monday night, he called Cathy and said to enroll the girls in school in Alexandria; they wouldn't be coming home for a while.

Sometime that day, a trooper had made it to Danny's neighborhood and told him the rainwater had only gotten to the level of the sidewalk, and that the house was fine. Danny thought he could relax and do his job. But the trooper couldn't see that it wasn't rain that was the problem: It was rising lake water. The next report Danny had about his house, the water on his first floor was up to three feet.

With other troopers, he drove down Claiborne Avenue in an elevated vehicle on loan from the military. They tried to rescue stranded nuns from the Ursuline Academy but were pushed back by deep water. A few blocks down Claiborne was the Memorial Medical Center, Tami's last stop before leaving the city. Doctors, nurses, and patients waited for days to be rescued; there would be allegations of mercy killings of some patients.

Back at the station, Danny worked the night shift, coordinating search-and-rescue teams from across the country. At two thirty each morning, he had a break and could talk to Cathy, who'd wait up for his call and take the phone out to a swing in front of her parents' house. Danny would ask what she'd been seeing on CNN; he had no other source of news. He had heard rumors of massive rioting, killings, and rapes, but didn't know what to believe. He told her about how he helped police the thousands of people who had been pulled off their rooftops and out of the water, and deposited on the Interstate 10/Causeway Interchange. In the middle of the night, he walked through the stench and felt the sweat pour down his body. He could only imagine what this place was like during the heat of midday. He looked at the old people, the families, the children, well aware that some wouldn't make it.

Claire titled the next e-mail "sugar," a family word for love. She wrote it at nine thirty at night on Wednesday, August 31:

> I love you and hop to see you soon and I'm not kidding
> CATTY is doing fine and we are to
> casey just had a little spell because she missed you
> and when she was crying, she was in Mommy's lap and
> mommy was crying to
> and I was about to cry
> and mommy isnt' getting much sleep
> well I think you get the point
> we are all ready to see you SOON
> love Claire

Danny received the message two days later and wrote back right away. "Tell everyone that I'm OK and I love them," he said. "I love you!!!!!" On Sunday, Cathy drove the girls down to Baton Rouge, to a seafood restaurant called Ralph & Kacoo's. The manager let them use a meeting room for the afternoon reunion with Danny. Cathy brought him food and new underwear. Danny's sister-in-law brought an iron and a sewing kit to hem his pants. "I'll never forget telling him good-bye that day," Cathy recalled.

Following the Sugarcane Academy parents' meeting at Audubon Park, Cathy had one more event to attend in New Orleans before heading back to Alexandria: her first departmental faculty meeting at Loyola, to discuss the January reopening of the university. While the children stayed with Danny in LaPlace, she joined her colleagues in a discussion about the issues facing Loyola, but she had trouble maintaining her composure. When the meeting ended, she quickly got up to leave. On her way out, she blurted out something about Sugarcane Academy, and how it looked like it didn't have a location, so she didn't know where she and her daughters were going to live.

"How many rooms do you need?" asked Mary Blue, also an associate professor in the communications department. "I've got three."

Mary Blue had taught at Loyola for twenty-five years and was there when the School of Mass Communications building was built. She called the fourth floor "my space," Cathy said. Everyone right on up to the president of the university knew that Mary Blue ruled the fourth floor. Cathy asked Kiki to write a proposal that Mary could show to her administrators. There wasn't time to wait for approval. Mary had all the keys to the doors. The word went out: As planned, Sugarcane Academy would reconvene after its one-week Halloween break at nine o'clock on Monday, November 7. All families were to report for morning meeting at a palm court outside the communications building at Loyola University.

When Monday came, a Loyola University campus policeman arrived to see children chasing each other around the walkways under palm trees and parents sitting on benches, casually drinking coffee. Cathy ran up to talk to him. "Campus is closed," the officer told her. Cathy bluffed. She said that they were waiting on approval. She didn't say they hadn't yet requested it. That night, Cathy sent an e-mail to the dean, the provost, and the Reverend Kevin Wildes, the university president. Mary called the next morning. She'd gotten a direct call from the president. He didn't ask about insurance. He had already heard about Sugarcane Academy. He told Mary that bringing the school to Loyola was the easiest decision he'd had to make since the storm.

The start of Sugarcane Academy in New Orleans brought a new rhythm to our lives. During the day, we visited friends, helped clean up or gut houses, argued with insurance adjusters, waited for contractors. In the afternoon, we waited for our children to emerge from the doors of Loyola's communications building. Kevin and Inta Phayer brought bags of po'boy sandwiches that didn't sell earlier in the day. We unwrapped the sandwiches and our kids burst through the doors.

They emerged as if one body. New games swept en masse across the kids. They devised a new way of walking, three at a time, with two kids supporting the third on their backs. They would lumber like baby dinosaurs across the lawn until they collapsed in laughter. Paul Reynaud walked through the doors behind them, carrying a large plastic bucket filled with pretzels or animal crackers. Kids dashed up, grabbed a handful, and kept on going.

By the middle of November, about fifty children were enrolled at Sugarcane Academy. Sometimes, new parents arrived without warning and dropped off kids; the teachers always took them in. Most children had been students at Lusher. A few came from other schools across the city. Some families showed up just for a day or two. During our first week back home, I had pulled down the previous year's first-grade class list from the refrigerator door. It included names and phone numbers; I called each number. Most weren't working, but I got in touch with Kayla Woods, a friend of Cecilia's who had evacuated to Houston. Kayla's family was coming back to New Orleans during the week before Thanksgiving. They dropped Kayla off at Sugarcane Academy and went out to their house in New Orleans East. I talked to her dad one afternoon, waiting for the kids to emerge from school. He had spent the entire day in their house and managed to salvage just one pair of cuff links from the wreckage. They didn't yet know if they would return to New Orleans to live.

The new version of the school was divided by grades and subject matter. Paul Reynaud and Lisa Sirgo taught kindergarten and first grade. Megan Neelis and Maureen Maloney took the second and third graders. Michele Barbier and Robin Delamatre taught the fourth through seventh graders. Elizabeth Kahn came in for reading and library, and Mark Hughes taught music. Sabrina Crais and Karen Good opened a preschool in a room adjoining Paul Reynaud's class. For recess, the classes would cross St. Charles Avenue to Audubon Park.

It was when they crossed St. Charles that Megan Neelis started noticing how the older kids would grab for the hands of the youngest kids. They even stayed near them to play. In her years of teaching, Megan had never seen this before. Some of the more troublesome kids—the ones that gave you the most grief—would wait patiently for the youngest kids to catch up.

We paid the teachers by asking each family to contribute fifty dollars a week if they could afford it. For some teachers, it was the only money they made that fall. Paul Reynaud soon took on the role of principal. He said it took him a while to bring the other teachers around to his philosophy of education, which included long recesses.

The teachers were given free rein to design their classes. Robin Delamatre and Michele Barbier wanted to keep the older kids in line with what other Louisiana students were studying. During the first week, they met to look through the state curriculum. They saw that there was a unit on migrations. "A couple days earlier in the *Times-Picayune*, they had a map called the Katrina Exodus," Robin said. "So we decided to talk about the history of diasporas." They studied voluntary migrations and forced migrations, and learned about the Acadians, the Trail of Tears, the California Gold Rush, the Irish Potato Famine, the northward black migration, the Dust Bowl, and Hurricane Katrina. The teachers hoped that the kids would see themselves as part of history. This might help them understand the specific pains that they, their friends, and their parents were feeling. "Whatever we were doing needed to be relevant to what was going on in their lives right now, at this moment," Robin said. "That became our mantra."

Cathy and Danny Franklin set up their home on the second floor of their house. The first floor was gutted, with sheets of plastic hanging where walls once stood. I stopped by one afternoon and we sat in the section of the main floor that had previously been their living room. Danny told me he had plunged in and gutted the house as soon as the waters went down. Some days, he said, he had a harder time than others. It's not easy to come home from work and see the insulation that needs fitting, the bricks that still need cleaning, the back fence that was still collapsed. New Orleans could be dispiriting.

Danny looked at the girls' piano, where before the evacuation Claire had practiced show tunes. It had sat submerged for days. He hit its keys and listened to the thudding sound, and wondered if it could be fixed. It was a good piano. He should get someone in to look at it. He added it to his list. "I'm not afraid to admit this, the main thing is the depression," he said. "You think about what's happened and what's going on and what you got to get rebuilt, and it can get to you sometimes."

Despite his earlier reservations about taking the girls out of school in Alexandria, he was glad to have them around. The other night, he said, they went to Audubon Park and played chase. He figured he made one too many sharp turns on the grass; by the end of the night, he had pulled his hamstring. He laughed at himself. "I haven't done that in a long time," he said.

In November 2005, the vast majority of the city still smelled like dead fish and old garbage. The new cityscape of yellowish brown waterlines and bright red search-and-rescue markings imprinted itself on your brain. You saw it again when you closed your eyes at night to sleep. You drove through the neighborhoods, tracking the progress of your personal landmarks. The first time I was in the city, I passed our favorite local ice cream store, Angelo Brocato's, its large sign crashed on the sidewalk in front of the store. Weeks later, I noticed that its display cases, once filled with tiramisu and Neapolitans and swans made of ice cream and pastry shells, were pushed to the curb, cracked and dirty. Old candy spilled out of filthy trays. In the weeks to follow, the shop stood quiet and boarded, betraying no secrets about its future.

Around it, the Mid-City neighborhood was in darkness. Most of the city was in darkness. Uptown became known as the Sliver by the River. We also called it, bitterly, the Isle of Denial, because you would attempt to forget what had happened for the length of a dinner, or a glass of wine, or a game of tag at the park. It could be an unbearable feeling to drive from lit-up neighborhoods into dark neighborhoods, and back again. In November, when people began putting up Christmas lights on the Uptown side of the chasm, the changeover from light to darkness became even more surreal.

One unforgettable November morning, the Audubon Zoo reopened. It was like a splinter of sunlight. The shiny elephant fountain shot water into the air as children were reunited with their favorite zoo animals. But we saw one friend walking silently behind his family. He'd lost his house, there were questions about his job, they were staying with relatives out of town, and it was wearing him down. "He's not doing well in all this," mutual friends told us.

In New Iberia, the children had named their new school after the surrounding sugarcane fields. But just what surrounded their school now?

One night during our first week back in New Orleans, I heard a phone message from Mark Morici, a doctor and one of Tami's coworkers at Treadway Pediatrics. Tami had been sleeping when Mark called. I didn't tell her about the message until the next day. After breakfast, she called him back. At some point, I realized that she was sobbing. I looked over to see that she was slumped down at the dining room table. Kent Treadway had killed himself. Kent's wife, Tyra, had discovered his body.

We drove to their house, not more than a dozen blocks from ours. Inside, you could still see dark water stains at the edges of the floorboards, where the flood had seeped in. Tyra stood at the bottom of the stairs. Her grown children stayed near her. She struggled to speak. Since the storm, she said, Kent had been working in the suburb of Metairie. For Kent, battling traffic to work in a suburb was like commuting to a distant planet. Since the flood, they had received phone calls daily from families asking to have their records transferred to the cities where they now lived. Each call was like losing another family member.

For years, Kent had suffered from debilitating back pain. The best he ever felt was when he was with his patients. The past two months, there had been no relief, Tyra said.

None of this could explain, for Tyra or for us, why the fifty-eight-year-old doctor with the silver hair and mischievous eyes was no longer living. In the fall of 2005 an epidemic of suicides in New Orleans was another untreated symptom of the flood. Even though the local newspaper didn't report them as suicides, everyone knew they were happening, and we knew there would be more to come.

"I was always happiest just being in his shadow," Tyra managed to say to us as we stood at the bottom of the stairs. She also said they were about to celebrate their thirty-third wedding anniversary.

The visitation took place in a funeral home in Metairie. A long line of friends and former patients stretched out into the parking lot. Treadway Pediatrics had flooded, but the photographs of patients that had lined the walls had somehow been salvaged. They were now placed throughout the funeral home, pictures of smiling children from an earlier New Orleans that, as November stretched on, seemed irretrievable.

Paul Reynaud stepped out onto Decatur Street and put on his sunglasses. He was wearing a plaid shirt, brown shoes, and dark green pants. He had placed six sharpened pencils in his shirt pocket and kept one in his hand. He began checking off names.

Forty-two children were running around, climbing on the parking-lot barriers around the Aquarium of the Americas, which hadn't yet reopened. After the flood, when the aquarium's generators ultimately gave out, ten thousand fish died in their tanks. But nobody mentioned this as the kids played outside. We were on Sugarcane Academy's field trip to the French Quarter.

We walked along Decatur Street, near a tent city for rescue teams that stood next to the Jax Brewery. A posted sign said the encampment was government property and off-limits to civilians. Blackwater Security workers guarded its entrance. We stopped in a parking lot and the children bunched around Paul. "Here's what you're doing today," he announced. "You're trying to look through what is here today to see what was behind it years ago. This used to not be a parking lot. People didn't drive cars. What was it? What's not here anymore?"

He looked around. "Right here on this block, this used to be a sugar exchange," he said. "It was developed by James Freret." He waved his hand while he talked. All along the street, he said, were buildings that once were used in the sugar industry..

He led the way up the street to Jax Brewery, a shopping mall that caters to tourists. "Now, this big building used to be a brewery. A beer factory. My grandfather worked there. You could come down here and they would be making beer all the time. You could smell it in the air."

"Did it smell good?" Claire Franklin asked. Paul nodded. He continued up Decatur and pointed to the St. Louis Cathedral. "What did it used to be?" he asked. "A church. What is it now? A church. That didn't change."

He told the children that years ago, soldiers used to march up and down Jackson Square. Then the soldiers were gone. Now the soldiers are back.

The next stop was Café du Monde, which had reopened on October 19. The kids filled the tables; when the beignets arrived, they blew off the powdered sugar until it clouded the air and coated their clothes. Paul next led them to Southern Candymakers, where they were all given small bags of pralines and chocolates. On the way out, they walked past a cigar store. Paul made a quick decision and turned into the shop. One of the older students protested. "There are little children here," he told Paul. But as men rolled cigars, Paul noted that this was one of the few places on the street where people still made things by hand.

Paul led the children across Decatur Street. Back in the parking lot, he offered one final lesson about looking at the old buildings. "Remember, you can look right through something and see what used to be there," he told the kids. "The same way, you can look at it and try to see it the way it might become. That's what we're trying to do today."

This was our assignment: Look hard enough at our city until we could somehow catch sight of its future.

CHAPTER 7

~~~~~~

In late November, I received a phone call from the Lafayette school district. The stories I had heard when I was in the Cajundome were true. A one-room schoolhouse had operated inside the shelter during the massive evacuation that rolled across the state and into Texas. Over a period of two months, an estimated 18,500 Louisianans had stayed at the Cajundome. At its peak, 7,000 evacuees camped out together inside its walls. And, the school district informed me, one of the people working there was Keith Bartlett, a teacher who had previously worked for five years at the New Orleans Alternative High School.

At my newspaper, we had reported on Alternative High School, which is where kids in New Orleans landed after they were kicked out of other schools. The reporter, Lili LeGardeur, had interviewed Bartlett, who told her that out of his class of nine kids, five had witnessed a murder. When the Lafayette school district gave me Keith's name, I asked Lili about him. "A wonderful man," she told me.

I called Keith, hoping to get a clearer picture of where New Orleans kids had landed and how they were doing. By the end of October, the Cajundome was no longer operating as a shelter. Keith told me that his work had shifted. He invited me to the Vermilion Conference Center in Lafayette to meet his team of three teachers. There, he'd explain more.

When I arrived at the Vermilion Center, Keith walked out of a long, paneled room to meet me in the parking lot. Three women walked behind him. One wore wire-rimmed glasses and a pressed, lime green jacket. I stared at her. I knew the face from another place and time: Anne Crow. My daughter's kindergarten reading teacher. Miss Anne taught Cecilia the difference between fiction and nonfiction, and showed her where to look in a book if you want to discover its birthday. Now she was in the Lafayette area, too.

Anne told me she had evacuated to Sulphur, Louisiana, where she had stayed for two weeks before moving to Lafayette. The district held a job fair for evacuated teachers. Although she didn't get an offer at the fair, she received a phone call a few days later. The voice on the other end asked if she'd like to meet at the Cajundome to discuss a different kind of teaching opportunity.

She told me this much, but there wasn't time to talk anymore. Anne and Keith—along with teachers Janie Malveaux and Linda Eubanks—were on the way to Westside Elementary

School in the nearby town of Scott. The school district counted 1,147 evacuated children still in its schools. Tests were showing that nearly half were struggling in the classrooms. The district had hired the New Orleans teachers to visit the schools and find out how they could be helped. The teachers gave themselves a title: Bridge Team.

Like most school buildings in the Lafayette area, Westside is a sprawling, one-story structure sitting on neatly kept grounds, with an attached playground. Walking inside, one of the first things I noticed was an art project displayed in one of its corridors. Students drew timelines of their lives, decorated with their own baby pictures, with photos of their parents, vacation photos, and school pictures of friends. But a few of the timelines on the wall were illustrated only with computer-generated line drawings of birthday cakes or faces or animals. These were the children who owned no photographs: the evacuees.

The school's principal, Carole Broussard, greeted the New Orleans teachers. Keith introduced himself with the tone of a doctor explaining his procedures. "We're going to take a little informal look at each of the thirty children that you have," he said. "We'll see what their basic needs are and then we'll bring the data back to the district and a program will be planned, and sorry that it's taken so long."

There was immediate confusion about lists of names. The

principal had prepared a list of evacuees who were having trouble with their classwork. The Bridge Team had a list of all the evacuated students in the school. The school didn't have that list and couldn't identify those students. "I couldn't tell you who's New Orleans, who's Lafayette," Carole said.

They compared lists some more, and Keith explained how the team liked to work: Three children would come into a room at a time. Anne Crow would be seated at one table to test reading skills. Janie Malveaux would sit at another table to check on math. And Linda Eubanks would talk with the children to see if they needed counseling.

Keith carried a folder that contained freshly minted "informal student assessment" sheets, on which the teachers could mark down how well the students were doing in language and math. There was a line in the evaluation called "storm information": In addition to New Orleans students, a few evacuees from Hurricane Rita also were at the school. Boxes could be checked to indicate Katrina or Rita, and other boxes were used to mark who evacuated prestorm and those who stayed during the flood.

The teachers coded all their notes by using different colored markers. An orange marker was for children who had suffered trauma related to one of the hurricanes. Orange came out when a child talked about seeing another child fall out of a boat and the adults just couldn't "flip him over fast enough." Or when they learned about a boy who didn't stop asking everyone who was going to visit New Orleans to look for a cat with spots. He had to leave that cat behind. Please, he asked, keep an eye out for a cat with spots.

The Westside principal nodded. "Three at a time," she said. "We'll bring in three of Miss Hypolite's. And Miss Hypolite is from New Orleans, she'd also like to meet you."

The rotations began, three children each cycle. The first group to arrive were three girls, each wearing a heavy jacket over her school uniform. "Ladies, I'm here with three of my friends, and all of us were chased out of New Orleans by this storm named Katrina," Keith said in the same soft explanatory tones he'd used with the principal. He told the girls that the school district hired the teachers to check on the kids, to see if they needed any kind of help. "You're not in trouble," he assured them.

Behind Keith, in a room decorated with bright posters advertising good judgment and teamwork, the three teachers sat at evenly spaced tables. At Linda Eubanks's table, a rocking chair was available for a child to sit in. At the far end of the room, Cynthia Bernard, the school counselor, sat at her desk and caught up on paperwork.

Over the next couple of hours, as students rotated through the room, I listened to the murmur of conversations, a mix of questions about the difference between fiction and nonfiction, or how to round off numbers, or floods. "We're not going back," said one girl with her ponytail pulled back into a white ribbon, as Janie nodded. I heard Anne ask another girl, "Are you able to concentrate in school?" The girl said that it was kind of hard. "Because you're thinking about other things?" Anne asked. The girl said yes. "We had to leave our cat," she said. "I don't know if he's okay."

Three by three they came in, again and again. I heard Janie repeat her own story to the children at her table. She seemed to know every neighborhood and every street the children listed. She told them about her own house, how it had flooded. The children answered her story with one of their own.

"My name is Miss Linda, and I'm going to talk with you about the storm, or whatever brought you here," Linda said to a boy who was melting into the rocking chair. "We stayed at a truck stop," the boy said. "I slept there. We left with my iguana named Herbie. But my bird and fish died. I should have saved them."

"Do you like the Transformers?" a boy asked Anne. She looked at him carefully and paused. "Medium," she said. "I'm not crazy about them." He said, "I go to the Planet Drool." She asked, "For make-believe fun?" He said, "For real fun." Anne made marks on the form as the boy talked excitedly about the movie characters Shark Boy and Lava Girl, and Mr. Electric, and how together they fight the hurricane. After the storm, he evacuated to Planet Drool, the boy said, making another reference to the movie. And after Planet Drool, he went to his mama's house.

When the boy was done at Anne's table, he started drawing superheroes. Keith told him it was time for his recess. The boy waved him off. "I'd rather draw," he said.

"When I was a little girl, that's just where I grew up," I heard Janie telling a girl. "Now, which of these numbers is 450 when rounded to the nearest 10, and 500 when rounded to the nearest 100? I'll give you a few minutes."

They kept coming, from Chalmette or the Ninth Ward or the West Bank, each carrying a portion of the hurricane and the grief.

After a while, I dropped to the back of the classroom. Cynthia Bernard had been a counselor at the school for the past ten years, and a teacher before that. She said that local parents were concerned at first about the influx of new children. She would just tell them, "Put yourself in that shoe." Then they all went to work, helping each kid get school uniforms of red, white, and blue shirts, and navy and khaki pants. A school in Minnesota sent money for the kids' coats, she said.

She spoke softly as a new group of girls entered the room. "These are some of our children who came right after the storm," she said. "They've been in a KOA campground in Scott." Cynthia told me how one girl said that her cousin had slipped off the roof. The water was rising. The cousin couldn't be reached. "She kept going back to, 'I lost a cousin. How could I lose a cousin?' And she said they have to go back and try to find her body."

I asked her how she gets children to talk about such things.

She pulled out a folder that was marked NEW ORLEANS. "They express how they feel in art," she said. "Then, when they talk, they're just talking about a picture. It offers a pass."

She opened the folder, which was filled with drawings. The first one was a simple picture of a house: a square topped by a triangle. But the triangle was tilted off the square, and a dark, horizontal line was scrawled through the center of the picture.

In another, a road grew smaller until it ended abruptly at a wall of dark, gray swirls.

I asked if the children talked about dreams. I told her that my four-year-old son woke up the previous night with a dream that he had been left behind. He said he had dreamed that the family had gone to a movie without him. Cynthia nodded. "The thing I notice the most is that none of them want to sleep alone," she said.

We paged through more drawings, some of which displayed children's faces with frowns and large teardrops. The children had been asked to write "feeling words" next to the drawings. You saw the same words, page after page. *Sad. Sorry. Angry. Hurt. Mad. Guilty.*

"You see this girl here." Cynthia looked up as a tiny girl sat down in the rocking chair to talk with Linda. Then she showed me a drawing by the same girl, a self-portrait of a girl standing in front of a house, with tears falling from her face in diagonal lines. "What do you notice here?" I asked.

"How big the house is," she said. "It's a big feeling."

———

As the last group of students left for recess, a woman quietly entered the room and introduced herself to Keith. Kim Hypolite had wanted to meet the teachers from New Orleans. She'd worked in New Orleans public schools for most of her twenty-six-year career. Most recently, she was principal at Lake Area Middle School. On Monday, September 12, she began teaching at Westside.

She told me that on the Saturday before the storm, she and her daughter had gone to the beauty parlor to get their hair done. Her sister called while she was there. "What are you doing?" her sister asked. "Getting my hair done," she replied. "It's Saturday."

She finally left town on Sunday morning with her extended family. When she saw footage of a flooded strip mall at Paris Avenue and Robert E. Lee Boulevard, she recognized the neighborhood surrounding her school, and she knew her job was gone. She met Westside principal Carole Broussard at the Lafayette job fair and accepted the job in Scott, a town she'd never heard of. Other teachers gave her mattresses and bed frames, pans and towels, and department-store gift certificates. She said she walked into the school that first day carrying nothing but a purse. "A purse!" she said again. Of all her memories of September 2005, the notion that she'd walk into a classroom without a curriculum, charts, and supplies seemed the most ludicrous.

She hadn't taught a class in sixteen years. Each one of the twelve students assigned to her on that first day was an evacuee from Hurricane Katrina. She knew this going in. Her job was to teach the children of the storm, and she felt grateful for this. Mothers came to the class, each holding a child by the hand. She promised she'd take care of them like her own. It helped when she told them she was from New Orleans.

Each child came into the class with a story. One family had enrolled their fourth-grade daughter at a local Catholic school that at first was offering free admission. But when the school said that the family would need to begin paying tuition, they found Westside. "Her mother was distraught about uprooting her child once again. I just approached her and said, 'Mom, we have fifteen other kids who left their school either once or twice. We're glad to have her.'" The girl's family had also recently located the body of a relative—the girl's aunt—who had died in the flood. The family was returning to New Orleans to fill out paperwork. A class assignment that day was writing descriptive paragraphs. "Her heart was with her family, so this is what the child wrote about," Kim recalled. "Her writing was very vivid, about what the aunt meant to her. She wanted to read it in the class. It was a silence, a hush, that fell over the room."

Kim never learned the details about the girl's aunt, but she believed that she hadn't evacuated, and that her remains were found in her home. A year ago, she said, the girl probably would have written her descriptive paragraph about her aunt's famous gumbo or cookies or pie. "I'm concerned that with young children—not just the children at Westside, but everywhere—that they've experienced some things that we've not even begun to tap into," she said.

Kim was glad the school put the evacuees into her classroom. With her, they wouldn't get lost in the shuffle.

As for her own story, she had lost her house on Bullard Avenue in New Orleans East; she lost all of her family pictures, her rosary beads, and her collection of crystal and porcelain elephants. On one trip back to New Orleans, she visited her old school. The gate was open and she drove over the dried, cracked sludge that covered the drive. The school's windows were blown out and debris was scattered across the yard. It had been a brand-new middle school for mostly poor children in the neighborhood, and it struggled academically. But in the two years since she started as its first principal, it had started showing progress. It had a winning volleyball team, a marching band with red jackets, and a $68,000 grant for the school's first library.

She said she thought of her school as a bud that was beginning to bloom.

Standing outside Lake Area Middle School, she peered through the window at the cafeteria freezer, which the rushing lake water had twisted off its foundation. The large deck where students sat after lunch was tossed to the side of the yard. She thought of all the teachers who came in early, stayed late, tutored, and tried to develop extracurricular programs. It was over. Kim drove back to Lafayette, where she was staying in a house filled with ten adults and two children. There was no privacy. "It was very difficult to cry," she said.

Sometimes, she said, she would be leading her class at Westside, and something about New Orleans might come up in discussion that hit her a certain way. She said she would just ask the kids to give her a minute, she'd be right back. Then she'd walk to the back of the room. Or she might make a quick trip to the drinking fountain. "And I come back and I'm okay and I'd say, 'All right, gang, number four is . . .'"

After leaving Westside, we drove back to the Vermilion Conference Center, where the four teachers would spend the afternoon sorting through the forms they'd checked off in the Scott school. But before getting started, they agreed to talk about their experiences in the Cajundome.

Keith Bartlett didn't know when the school district started thinking about conducting classes at the Cajundome. "I was in Opelousas and into my own misery at that time," he said.

"My first question was, why were they doing it?" Anne said of the shelter school. The district had already placed thousands of children into area elementary, middle, and high schools. It was providing bus service to and from the Dome. But many parents wouldn't let their kids board a bus to a strange school in a strange town. Others didn't know how long they would stay in the area. To serve these parents, the district opened what it called a "transition school."

Anne remembered that it took her a while to negotiate the process of being admitted into the Cajundome. After she made it through the gates, she located Keith in the crowd. He hired her on the spot. He interviewed Janie in the Cajundome lobby and hired her, too.

On Monday, September 19—three weeks after the flood—the school was announced over the Cajundome loudspeakers. A teacher's aide was hired; she was living in the Dome and helped gather children for the classes. The teachers started kids off on art and reading and math. The school district provided backpacks, supplies, and awards for good work. There were morning classes for young children and afternoon classes for the older kids. The teachers remembered how the children clung to them. "You could feel the need," Janie said.

"There was one little girl, I think she went on to Texas," Janie said. "A sweet little girl. A bright student. When she talked to me about what she lost, I told her about what I lost. But when Hurricane Rita came up, she asked me, 'What do you think I should do, Miss Janie? What do you think the storm is going to do?' She was concerned about her whole family. 'Sweetheart, I don't know. We'll just wait and see.'"

Anne remembered a little boy who would throw his books around the room, disrupting reading lessons. She asked him what he was mad about. He wouldn't talk; he would only kick and throw books. But another kid in the class told her that the boy's mother had just left the Cajundome for Houston to find his sister. He'd stayed up late that night crying. "I said, 'You're fine. You have a right to be angry. You cannot hurt anyone else. But if you want to just put your head down on your desk, fine.'"

That's how a school day could go in the Cajundome. There was sadness in her own family, Anne said. Her parents had lost their house of sixty years. "But that's a different kind of sad," Anne said. "We were staying in a support group, a twelve-person-strong household. I needed to help children. That's about the only thing I could do. I didn't want to just feel. I wanted to be able to do."

So she did puppets, constructed from brightly colored bags she bought at Wal-Mart. The kids in kindergarten loved making puppets. The first and second graders could use the puppets to learn about characterization and moods and tones. "It's easily done," said Anne.

As she talked, I heard the voice of the teacher who once had captivated my own child. "They were stressed kids," Anne said. "If someone poked them, they were uptight. They were sleeping in cots next to each other. All kinds of things were seen. They told us about it all."

Mainly, she said, she believed that her job was to listen to the kids. Anne thought about what the children likely heard their parents talking about in the next cot over. She remembered when she was a child during the Cuban missile crisis, listening in terror as her parents talked about what the family would do in case of an attack during the school day. "That kept coming back to me, because I was so petrified," she remembered. "It terrified me, thinking that they were going to let me go on a bus, and I could hear my father saying, 'We would never see them again.' Those words, 'never see again.'

"And that's how those kids must have felt, too. They were mixed up."

At the Vermilion Conference Center, the teachers talked for a while about the idea of closure. It was a word you heard a lot in New Orleans after the flood. "Most of the children haven't gone back to see their house," Anne said. "Or their toys destroyed. I wonder if closure is necessary."

Janie and her husband were debating bringing their own daughters back to New Orleans to see their flooded house. Janie wanted them home for Christmas. They could stay in a hotel. She thought it was important to visit her daughter's old bedroom. Janie and her husband had purchased a collection of wicker furniture for her as a reward for graduating from high school with honors. Janie thought her daughter needed to see for herself that the furniture was gone.

Janie said that when the news of the flood hit her, she could barely get out of bed. She was one year away from retiring. Her house was filled with the accumulated memories of thirty-eight years of marriage. "When Anne told Keith about me, I knew this was God's way of getting me going," she said. "Because I couldn't have made it otherwise. Watching the kids, when you saw them look at you with a smile, then you felt okay. You had a reason to be there."

At the end of September, when the Cajundome was evacuated for Hurricane Rita, the school in the shelter closed even more quickly than it had opened. The teachers were conducting class when they got the call. Officials asked them to keep on with their lessons, to give their parents time to pack. As parents and workers and guards hurried about, Anne and Janie froze in place and continued discussing fractions and synonyms. Then Anne began to collect books for the children to bring on the buses. She encouraged the older children to read to the younger kids. "They were beautiful," Janie remembered. "They were so cooperative. They'd say, 'I'm going to read this to so-and-so!' But inside, my heart was breaking for them."

After Hurricane Rita hit the coast, the Cajundome served as a shelter for evacuees from both storms. The teachers returned to find that their classroom was now needed for other purposes, and all their supplies had been stuffed onto a single service cart. They picked up the pieces and set up a school at a facility a mile from the Cajundome. The first day, one student showed up. Over the next few days, more arrived. They never saw many of their kids from the first weeks again. But every once in a while, as they made the rounds to schools in the area, a Cajundome student would show up in a new doorway to greet them, now part of a group of three to be assessed for math, reading, and counseling.

As the afternoon at the Vermilion Center wore on, the teachers turned to their forms and their color-coded markings.

Keith wasn't sure what exactly the three teachers would do next after completing the assessments in each school in the district. The teachers wanted to set up facilities as close to the students as possible, to help them with whatever they needed. Beyond that, they didn't really know their own plans. They didn't know if they were returning to New Orleans, or if they would have jobs past the end of the school year. "You do what you can do," said Janie.

CHAPTER 8

When I first visited St. Bernard Parish after the hurricane, I couldn't imagine ever bringing children there. I never thought I'd bring a child of my own.

I saw just two young girls that day in mid-September, playing on a field that looked scorched. Their father stood nearby with an absent look in his eyes. Hundreds of people were converging on a government complex in Chalmette. There were reports that a parishwide town-hall meeting would take place at ten o'clock in the morning. It would be the largest gathering of St. Bernard Parish residents since the storm.

Everywhere you looked there was devastation. On August 29, a storm surge pulsed directly from the Gulf through the Mississippi River–Gulf Outlet Canal. Water poured in from Lake Borgne from the northeast, topping the 40-Arpent Canal. From the west, it crashed through the Industrial Canal.

Every home and business in the parish, which is adjacent to New Orleans, just east of the Lower Ninth Ward along the Mississippi River, was flooded.

When the flood finally receded, St. Bernard looked like it had suffered through every disaster imaginable. The cracked mosaic of mud was the landscape of a drought. Shredded brick walls and overturned cars were scenes from a war zone. The vegetation appeared charred, as if from a massive fire.

Some stories that came out of St. Bernard during Katrina were horrific, none more so than that of St. Rita's Nursing Home. Thirty-four residents died, many bedridden and helpless as the water rose quickly, blanketing their bodies and covering their faces.

Immediately following the hurricane, Henry "Junior" Rodriguez, the parish president, called St. Bernard the next Love Canal, referring to the infamous New York State toxic landfill. That's because the floodwaters pushed a tank at the Murphy Oil plant off its foundation. Eight hundred thousand gallons of oil emptied into the floodwater, according to official estimates. It was carried through neighborhoods and into homes. In much of St. Bernard, the mud wasn't brown, like it was in other places that flooded heavily. It was black, like charcoal. The waterlines on buildings in the vicinity of Murphy Oil looked like smears of ink.

Many peoples' ruined houses now bore painted messages, like giant postcards. Some gave new phone numbers, so friends could find one another. Some swore to return, while others bore bitter good-byes like "Thanks FEMA Murphy Oil Bush Brown" scrawled across a garage door, with the added sentence "You work fast" and an arrow pointing to the contaminated ground. "Mr. Bush where are you sleeping tonight?" was scrawled across a line of broken fence posts standing in front of another empty home.

St. Bernard Parish was about a half-hour drive from my own house. Before Katrina, I'd go there mainly for festivals; the towns that dot the parish are known for signature oyster, shrimp, and crawfish festivals. We'd also come out to get chocolate cake at Flour Power, which was Tami's favorite bakery. And just before the hurricane, Olivia Huston had her ninth birthday party at Skate World in Chalmette.

I was there just a few weeks after the flood receded to report on the environmental group Louisiana Bucket Brigade, which was investigating the Murphy Oil spill. We approached the St. Bernard government complex. The town meeting was largely advertised by word of mouth. Few people currently lived in the parish, but hundreds of cars lined the streets. As we drew near, we passed an old Wal-Mart parking lot, now filled with tents where you could go for hot meals, canned food donations, and medical care.

We approached to hear a roar of voices erupt from the council chambers, now a dusty, gutted concrete auditorium. We moved closer to see a crowd of about a thousand people. Some residents perched on empty window frames, cupping their ears to hear. At the outer edges, we could discern just a few random words coming from inside. Then a faint, rhythmic murmur rose up.

"We can't hear," screamed a woman from the back, standing on an ice chest.

"Shut up, we're saying the Pledge," shouted a voice from inside.

Peering over rows of heads, I could see a few figures on a stage, mostly men in shirtsleeves and ties. Sheriff's deputies lined the walls. A single folding chair and a microphone sat on the floor, facing the stage. It wasn't a town-hall meeting; it was a hearing. The man at the table was a state senator. After the Pledge of Allegiance ended, he began querying various officials in a voice that came out tinny and garbled, amplified only through two small speakers that were held by assistants at the sides of the stage. People pressed forward from the back to hear. More shouts were heard from the hundreds who were out of earshot.

"We lost our tax base here in St. Bernard Parish," one man in a suit told the senator. "Really!" shouted an old man in the crowd, getting up to leave. There was an announcement that the meeting would go on for eight more hours. People started to shout louder. Then parish president Junior Rodriguez, a bulky man with thick white hair, lifted up a gold-capped cane and slammed it down three times on the table in front of him. "Goddamn it, shut up!" he bellowed hoarsely at the crowd.

There was a hush, but it didn't last long. Officials took their turns at the hearing, each one seated in the folding chair with his back to the thousand residents. Congressional aides sat at the table, typing into laptops, their faces blank as slates. Only a few intelligible phrases squeaked out over the speakers: "All of our lives are at stake . . . You can never talk to the same person twice . . . Loan us money? It's a damn slap in the face to loan us money . . ."

A woman next to me said she was a lifelong St. Bernard Parish resident and she drove in from Dallas for this meeting. Now she was turning around and going back. "I need some information," she said. "I'm not going to get it here."

In early December, three months after the hearing, the houses in St. Bernard were still decimated. But a few now were decorated with old plastic Santas, some dressed in military fatigues and gas masks. "I feel like every time someone comes down I want them to drive the distance," Ronda DeForest told me. "Sometimes, I guess, I push it down their throats."

Ronda was driving me to her house in the Cypress Gardens neighborhood. She and her husband, Doyle, moved here nearly eight years earlier. At the time, their daughter, Isabella, was one year old, and Ronda was pregnant with their son, Paxton.

Ronda and Doyle owned the Flour Power bakery. One morning after dropping our kids off at Sugarcane Academy, my wife and I decided to drive through Chalmette. We stopped at the bakery to see how it had fared. As we peered through the dusty windows, we heard a cheerful voice. "Can I help you?" said Ronda, emerging from a white FEMA trailer next to their shop.

A few days later, I returned to talk more with the De-Forests. Ronda suggested we start with a drive. So we entered her old neighborhood, now a silent panorama. Evidence of human activity was limited to one giant crane that was moving debris. We passed a Buick that was balanced at a forty-five-degree angle, one back wheel on a house's roof, the other on top of the attached garage. Ronda pointed out a foundation with front stairs that led up to nothing except a toilet.

About a block away, a seemingly perfect house now sat in the middle of the road. The first time they saw it, Ronda said, someone had laid out a pair of black rubber shrimp boots as if they were sticking out from beneath the house, like the wicked witch from *The Wizard of Oz*. "You get to a point where you cry, you cry, you cry, and then, okay, we got to make the best of it now," Ronda said.

The yard around their own home was strewn with new two-liter bottles of soda and packages of unopened deodorant that they figured must have washed over from the Dollar General down the street. Videos and DVDs drifted over from a Blockbuster two blocks away.

For a week, cars and boats and sheds and houses had knocked around in this neighborhood like bathtub toys. "People who stayed, they're cooking pancakes in the kitchen, the next thing they know they're looking out the window and there's a ten-foot wall of water coming at them," Ronda said.

They didn't bring the kids the first time they returned. All Doyle wanted out of the house was his T-shirt collection. They fought through fallen furniture to reach their kitchen, where Ronda located her grandmother's recipe book. Doyle dug into the kitchen floor until he found her cobalt blue glass fleur-de-lis that had fallen from above the doorway. It wasn't broken. Because of moments like that, Ronda frequently talked about how lucky they were.

Now, she said, her house was slowly decaying; each time she returned, she noticed another object that had crashed to the floor. She carefully led the way to Isabella's room. Pink and lavender latex paint peeled off the walls like bark from a tree. The blades of the ceiling fan drooped down from the center base. Ronda never knew that ceiling fans could melt. When she first walked into this room, her first thought was of a weeping willow.

She pointed to a rotting canvas chair in the debris. All through the evacuation, Isabella kept talking about her purple butterfly chair. She couldn't understand why they couldn't go back and get it. That's when Ronda and Doyle decided to bring their children back to the house. They all put on face masks and rubber boots. The kids didn't burst into tears, Ronda said. They were simply awestruck.

Later on, Isabella had a nightmare about the hurricane. She sometimes asked about the next storm. Paxton was mostly concerned about the fate of his turtle, Franklina, who had lived in an aquarium on a chest of drawers, and was now gone.

Ronda grew up in this area. The DeForests had evacuated to northern Louisiana, where Doyle had spent much of his childhood. People were friendly there. But Isabella came home from her first day at the new school with questions about the practice of corporal punishment. Ronda thought spanking was illegal in Louisiana. She found out otherwise. At her children's new school, it was done under strict supervision, three times with a wooden paddle.

So when they heard about a new school for St. Bernard kids, they decided it was time to return home. The school was at the site of Chalmette High School. They visited it on November 14, the first day of classes. Ronda and Doyle saw their old principal and other teachers, and they heard the screaming of kids finding old friends, and were caught up in a rapture of hugging. "It was clear that this is absolutely where we need to be, no question," Doyle said. "It was our turning point. As we started driving back, we started talking. We said, we could do this. Apply for our own FEMA trailer. Try to get our own thing going."

This was what St. Bernard Parish officials hoped the school would accomplish: to bring families and businesses back to a place that once seemed hopeless.

After the flood, the first report from St. Bernard Parish was that its entire school district would close for the remainder of the academic year. The reasons were obvious: All fifteen schools had flooded. The parish's 8,800 public school students were scattered throughout Louisiana and across the country. Every child's home was uninhabitable. Nobody knew how far or how deep the 800,000 gallons of oil had seeped into the environment.

Doris Voitier, the district superintendent, had ridden out the storm in Chalmette High School. With Wayne Warner, the high school's principal, she helped ration the available food: drinking water, Froot Loops, and slices of bread. As water rushed in below, they pulled hundreds of their neighbors in through an open school window to a better place on the school's second floor.

Days passed with no contact from the outside world. It seemed that nobody knew they were there. Eventually, hundreds walked out through the water to the levees. Boats finally arrived for the others. The superintendent took one of these boats to safety in Baton Rouge. In October, she announced that the district would resume classes on the high school grounds. She relied on state and federal environmental agencies to verify that the area was safe for children. Because every single student was now homeless, free lunch would be provided for all. There would be after-school programs. The K–12 St. Bernard Unified School was born.

During one of my visits to the St. Bernard Unified School, I talked with two school administrators. They spoke proudly about the Chalmette Charmers, the high school dance team that received national honors each year. One woman told me about an award-winning academic games team. It was scattered in the evacuation, but four members met up at a competition. They called themselves Chalmette High, and they won. The other woman broke down at this news. She hadn't heard about that, she said. "It's been a hard day," she said, reaching for more Kleenex. "That's where you're catching me this morning."

I also met Lee Anne Harlton, who became site administrator for the elementary portion of the Unified School. Formerly, she was principal of Joseph J. Davies Elementary School, where Isabella and Paxton had been enrolled. She, too, had evacuated to Chalmette High School, and then moved to the Southwest Louisiana town of Crowley, where she had made her husband miserable until they decided to come home, she said. The first time she saw her old school after the storm, she looked at a massive hole torn into one corner. That was her office. She wanted to go in. She wanted closure. But the word *snakes* was written across the outside wall.

"These people had a horrible time with it, and they weren't on the news," she said, echoing the widespread belief that the media never focused adequately on St. Bernard Parish. "It's a forgotten place."

The first day of school, the children came in with stories about riding out the storm at the Domino sugar factory or on their daddy's oyster boat. They drew pictures, wrote stories, made videos. Immediately, counselors started meeting with groups and individuals.

By early December, more than six hundred children attended classes in a neat collection of modular buildings. Wooden porches framed the school; near the door were United States and Louisiana flags and a sign that read THE ST. BERNARD UNIFIED SCHOOL WELCOMES OUR STUDENTS HOME. Nearby, a large white tent with clear plastic windows served as the cafeteria. Across the street, rows of FEMA trailers would provide teacher housing. Lee Anne Harlton hoped to reside in one of the trailers. Of the eighty-two faculty and staff members at Davies Elementary, she told me, eighty of them lost everything they owned.

But that was the story everywhere in St. Bernard Parish. To prepare for the opening of the Unified School, Doris Voitier attended a series of meetings with a rotating cast of various heads of federal agencies. The only promise that she could elicit from anyone came from the Army Corps of Engineers, which told her it might be able to provide portable buildings by March 2006. That would wash out the school year, along with everything else. Her defiant reply is now the stuff of parish legend: "We'll do it ourselves and send you the bill!"

The results of the decision to open the school could be seen throughout St. Bernard Parish in places like the DeForest FEMA trailer. On a weekday morning in December 2005,

Isabella and Paxton were walking through the trailer, getting ready for school. Doyle had spent the previous evening digging through the muck of their house, looking for eyeglasses. Paxton had lost a screw from his glasses. In St. Bernard Parish, there were no longer any stores that stocked eyeglass screws or much else. So Doyle went diving through the debris for a pair of glasses. While he was there, he also found one of Paxton's green Joseph Davies school sweatshirts. The shirt didn't even smell like the flood.

On his way back to the trailer, Doyle told Paxton, he passed an enormous turtle in the road. He thought for a second about bringing it back. But there was no room in the trailer. Doyle told Paxton that it looked like Franklina. She looked healthy, he told his son.

The DeForests were doing most of the work on their bakery by themselves. The most difficult job would be emptying the walk-in cooler, which hadn't been opened since the storm. It was filled with milk and eggs. One company wanted $9,800 to do the job. The amount would exhaust the last of their insurance money.

Flies were thick outside. Every time a house was gutted, it added to the debris piles. Ronda and Doyle kept reminding their kids to use the hand sanitizer. They were figuring out how to reopen their bakery. Just thinking about it brought up reminders of what their community had lost. St. Rita's Nursing Home residents had been their customers, Ronda told me. When the bakery reopens, they would miss them even more.

But she also said that when their shop opened, it would be a place where you could close the curtains, and for an hour at least, a customer could escape what surrounded them day and night. The DeForests would even get the dinner theater going again, she vowed.

Grabbing her bookbag, Isabella said she liked the St. Bernard school better than the one in northern Louisiana. "Because they don't paddle us here," she said. "And I knew I was going to see some of my friends, and I did."

Moving was never really an option, Ronda said. "If they could find everyone in St. Bernard a big huge plot of land to go to and stay and rebuild, so we could all be together, I'd say do it. What makes this place special is not this house; it was the community. So that's my take on it. I would be happy wherever you stick me—as long as these people are the ones around me."

Occasionally, their children brought up the topic of the next storm. "We don't want to hide the fact that this could definitely happen again," Doyle said. "We talk to them like adults. And we tell them, life is an adventure. They understand. They're cool kids."

Students noisily filed into a makeshift auditorium and sat in folding chairs. Some wore basketball uniforms; others were dressed in khakis. This December afternoon was set aside for an after-school performance by Shine Productions, a St. Bernard Parish–based theater company that was founded by Barry Lemoine, a high school journalism and theater teacher. Years earlier, he conceived of a production titled *An Evening with Betsy,* based on oral histories of the 1965 flood; it was a hit on local stages in 2001. He was currently adapting it for Hurricane Katrina.

Shine Productions staged dinner theater shows at the Flour Power bakery; the DeForests told me about this production at the school. At first, I hoped I might bring Sugarcane Academy to the St. Bernard Parish school to see the play, as a field trip. But the production wasn't designed for younger kids. So after I checked it out with Unified School, I asked Kiki Huston if Olivia would want to come to the performance with Cecilia. Tami and I picked up the girls at Sugarcane Academy and drove to Chalmette.

Olivia and some friends had recently taken to wearing face masks—the ones that people used when they gutted houses—as fashion accessories. But when we started the drive to St. Bernard Parish, she grew quiet. Crossing the Industrial Canal into the Lower Ninth Ward, we could see a giant red barge that had burst through the levee. It now rested atop a school bus.

Cecilia marveled out loud at the spiderweb patterns on shattered car glass, and the bizarre appearance of overturned cars and blown-apart houses. "It's not cool, Cecilia," Olivia said, growing upset. "People lived there."

I didn't know what to say. I wondered if I had done something terribly wrong. We brought two children to a place that we didn't understand ourselves. Had we prepared them enough? I thought about how Mr. Reynaud would respond. I recalled the story about how, at a funeral, he had walked just a few paces behind a nephew, letting the child explore at his own pace, just being there if needed. I decided that I would let the scenes speak for themselves. I'd listen for questions.

There were none. We passed other local landmarks, including the now-desolate rink where we had all been roller-skating at Olivia's birthday party just months earlier.

Arriving at the school, we took our seats on the side, next to the Unified students. The kids applauded as Barry Lemoine entered the stage area from behind a curtain. "This is a new program. You're going to be the first ones to be able to see it, called *Voices from the Storm,*" he announced. The students cheered loudly.

"My brother was seven and my sister was five," he began. "Which means my parents were about fifteen years younger than I am right now. We lived in the Lower Ninth Ward. You all know where the Ninth Ward is.

"As Betsy's raging water rose, our family of five had to take safety up in the attic. And Princess, our German shepherd, was left on the kitchen table to fend for herself. The water was up to six feet and our family of five was huddled in the attic while our dog struggled for balance on top of that table. And when the boats came to get us, we had to leave Princess behind. And even as a kid I knew that something was the matter. How could they do that? How could the family pet be left behind like that?

"But what's even harder for me to grasp is what else was going through my parents' minds on that September night forty years ago, when the black water barged through the floor and invaded our homes, invaded our lives. My parents, they were just starting out life, and they made the choices that saved our lives. How can I question that?

"I was two. My brother was seven. My sister was five. And for five days we had to leave our homes, our lives, and our dog. And when we returned, all was lost. Cards, photo albums, everything. Everything except for a floor polisher that we found up in the attic." He paused. "And a German shepherd named Princess who was still on that table, wagging her tail, barking, as if to say, 'Hey, welcome back to your mildewed lives.'"

The students laughed. I could feel the relief in the room. "You know," Barry continued, "I don't know what the age of consciousness is or when we have our very first lasting memory, but for me it was seeing Princess on that kitchen table. I was two, and a memory was born."

That story was a true one, he said. When he first presented this play to young audiences, they had not experienced a hurricane. This time, everyone in the room had his or her own story. I looked at Olivia and Cecilia, and at the St. Bernard kids. They all sat quietly, paying close attention. Some of the monologues that followed were terrifying. An actress recounted the story of a girl who stood in water up to her chest, holding on to her sobbing father while her grandfather tied floating caskets to the church fence. Other segments featured the kinds of stock comic characters that, for many, defined St. Bernard Parish in the years between Betsy and Katrina. There were heavy accents and lines about "erster po'boys." A woman in a housecoat joked about "the best six years of her life" at Chalmette High.

The final monologue came from an interview with a woman whose parents went out in a boat the night Betsy hit. A stepbrother took the children to safety. Before her father left, the narrator—then a young girl—helped him put on his socks and shoes. Years later, she would learn that the remains of a body were found. She identified her father by the socks.

Concluded Barry: "You are our faith, you are our future, you are the voices of this storm."

We took the same route out of St. Bernard Parish, past the cars, the houses, the barge. Later, I learned from Kiki that Olivia cried herself to sleep that night.

CHAPTER 9

~~~~~~

In early December, we began planning a Sugarcane Academy trip to the Ogden Museum of Southern Art, in New Orleans' Warehouse District. Only open for two years before the storm, the Ogden was devoted to regional art and artists, and was located in a bright, contemporary building that made it a favorite for school field trips. When it reopened its doors on October 27, it became one of the first cultural institutions in New Orleans to start up after the flood. It scheduled concerts with musicians who had made it back, and it organized exhibits about the future of the city. But the Ogden hadn't yet had a field trip come through its doors.

We became the first. One museum volunteer told me that before the kids arrived, the staff took a morning walk through the galleries that now featured hurricane-related work. They wanted to make sure that if anybody was going to break down when they saw the art, they wouldn't do it in front of the children.

Photographer David Rae Morris had agreed to meet the kids in the gallery that displayed photos he'd taken in the weeks following the flood. Kids began filing into the room and looking at the pictures, some of which were graphic. In one, an eighty-six-year-old woman, dressed in slippers and a housecoat, wailed as she finally evacuated her house after the flood. In another, an Oregon National Guard unit marched down St. Claude Avenue; the boyish face of the lead guardsman plainly registered his shock. One picture showed a stray German shepherd standing in front of a downed street sign and ruined homes. Another had only a single row of white picket fence posts poking out of oily water.

Sugarcane's youngest kids were the first group in the gallery. They sat down on the floor around David Rae, who told them about September and how he had spent the month driving back and forth between his house in New Orleans and Jackson, Mississippi, to where he'd evacuated with his partner, Susanne Dietzel, and their three-year-old daughter, Uma. He talked about how crazy and dangerous it felt to be in New Orleans during that time. When he went back to Jackson, his daughter would look at the pictures he was editing and ask, "Papa, is that the storm?" She'd then settle down next to him to draw her own flood pictures. "We decided early on not to try to keep anything from Uma," David Rae told me later.

The children first wanted to know about David Rae's picture of the German shepherd. A volunteer at the museum told them about how people rounded up animals to bring to shelters or to return to their owners. Then they wanted to know about some of his more abstract photos, of the fence posts in the water, or the patterns of cracked sludge that were left by the receding water.

"What's that?" a girl asked, pointing to the fence posts.

"I stood on a ladder to take that picture," David Rae said. "It's a fence in the floodwater." He added, "I thought it looked pretty."

This provoked some discussion among the kids. "Sometimes you can find beautiful things in something that isn't beautiful at all," David Rae said. The children seemed to agree.

Eli Poche pointed to another picture. "Is that a house on the edge of a cliff?" he asked.

"No, that's a cemetery. The water got so high that some of the caskets came out of the tombs."

"How many?"

"I saw a lot."

"Did any dead people come out?"

"I didn't see any."

The kids eventually filed out and the next group was the older Sugarcane students; fourth and fifth graders now surrounded David Rae. Without warning, the conversation turned grim. One boy said he found a coffin in the graveyard.

There were two bodies in it. "One of my mom's cousin's friends got murdered in her house," one girl said. Another child talked about seeing a baby that floated away.

David Rae wasn't sure how to respond. He thought about how storm rumors had spread everywhere in the months after Katrina; there's no reason children should be immune. He paused to consider his options. "That's horrible," he finally said.

Olivia and Kiki Huston stood in the back of the gallery. Olivia pointed to a photograph of a man wearing military pants and holding a .22 rifle. He was sitting on a front stoop. The caption read that it was his grandmother's home. "Mommy, is he protecting his grandmother's house?" Olivia asked.

"Just from some people," Kiki said, not wanting to talk about it further.

Olivia and I walked around the gallery for a while. She told me about a recent trip she'd taken to Lakeview. She went to a friend's house that was filled with mold. "The last time I'd been there, we had a sleepover and we baked cookies in the kitchen," she said.

While the older kids stayed in the photo gallery, I joined the younger children upstairs, where the museum had an exhibit of paintings by Georgia-born artist Benny Andrews. Before the hurricane, Andrews had launched The Migrant Series, which included paintings inspired by the Dust Bowl migration. Following Katrina, he started working on paintings inspired by the Trail of Tears.

The children had been given pencils and paper. They sat on the floor beneath depictions of thin adults and hunched children walking along a dusty road.

"Stories about migrations were passed down from ancestor to ancestor," a museum volunteer was telling the children when I walked in. "Have you ever thought about how you are going to be the ancestors? What stories will you tell?"

Casey Franklin spoke up. "About our house," she said. "And how it's . . ." She lost the sentence and giggled, knocking her head with her fist.

I looked at the pictures the children were drawing. Some had the same squares and triangles, the broken houses in floods, that I'd seen in other children's drawings. There were also rows of cars, some rounded like the tops of eggshells, each with one square window, all in the midst of the evacuation.

Teachers were drawing, too. Natalie Maloney taught art at Sugarcane Academy and had been working with her class on making Mardi Gras cards, in an effort to get students thinking about the symbols of New Orleans. She now sat against a wall working on her own drawing. The dark outline of her own handprint covered scenes of the French Quarter and the Superdome.

Paul Reynaud sat cross-legged in the center of the room, concentrating on his own drawing. I looked over at his piece of paper. It showed the day back in New Iberia when, during an endless afternoon bayou recess, Callie Huston fell in the water. He'd written out a title: *The Pier Where We Went Fish-*

ing in New Iberia. There was a tree and a pelican on a stump. His final addition was a sketch of two little legs sticking straight out of the bayou.

At the front desk of the Ogden Museum, I picked up a small flyer announcing that the museum would host a weekend art activity for adults and children. It was titled The Power of Symbol, and would be led by a group called the Category 5 Artists. Participants could invent new designs based on the red *X* that was painted on their homes.

On Saturday, Tami and I brought our children to meet up with other families at the Ogden. Cecilia's friend Mitzi immediately sat on the floor. Miles joined her. They began placing dry red beans, rice, coffee, and other Louisiana products into a giant outline of a mandala. Cecilia went to a table where she drew on a sheet of paper that was divided into four quadrants and labeled THE MARK OF RECOVERY. The back of the page listed symbols from various traditions. Cecilia chose a symbol of strength. Then she drew a cluster of smiling faces and wrote out "Sugarcane Academy" in one quadrant.

A local organization called KIDsmART sponsored the three Category 5 artists who had set up the projects: Anne Cushwa, Ruth Robbins, and Geryll Robbins. Ruth told me how they were all studying in Peru when they learned that New Orleans was flooding. They went to a hospital to follow the news. They were joined there by travelers from around the world.

"We were in a hospital watching CNN," she recalled. "Everyone had a different reaction. The Israelis were like, 'The army's going to come in and evacuate everyone.' The British people were telling us that the army was just waiting for the storm to pass. The Peruvians just couldn't believe there were poor people in America, period. They couldn't believe those were American citizens they were seeing. But I just told them that I knew there wasn't going to be any help coming."

Like other teachers I knew, Ruth peered at the broadcasts and searched for kids she had previously taught. She'd worked in several New Orleans public schools, most recently at Fischer Elementary. When she returned to New Orleans after the flood, she heard rumors that the school might be open. But when she went to the school, it was still closed. She didn't know where her students were, but she thought she might see some of them soon, she said. The three artists were driving to Houston to work in a school that had started up since the evacuation. Nearly the entire population of students—more than three hundred kids—were from New Orleans. The school was called New Orleans West.

The artists agreed to meet me in Houston, and I set out on the six-hour drive across Louisiana. On the way, I thought of the images I'd seen all fall of children's art after the flood. A square box. Then a triangle. A blue line zigzagged across the page. Sometimes, the triangle was falling off the box. Or there was no box at all. Or the line was straight and covered with hard-pressed scribbles.

How many of these new cityscapes were being carried around in the heads of children? In Louisiana alone, state officials said that nearly 190,000 students were displaced because of the flood. Each brought along the details of their home, the water, evacuation.

The profession of art therapy has been around since the 1940s, according to the American Art Therapy Association. Art therapists work with children who might not have the words to describe what they have seen and what they feel. Despite the obvious need, there was no coordinated effort to use art therapy to help all the children after the flood. Private groups tried to fill in the gaps. Many children received no attention at all. But unpaid therapists and untrained volunteers did what they could.

One group visited the bleak FEMA trailer park in Baker, Louisiana, that now had been given the Orwellian name of Renaissance Village. FEMA had provided no play areas or after-school activities for the park's children. Therapists met children in a structure that had neither lights nor heat, reported Karla Leopold on a Web site for Rosie O'Donnell's For All Kids Foundation, which funded the visits. They worked with upwards of forty kids a day. The children filled the tables with drawings. At one point, the children at Renaissance Village created a city with cardboard boxes. It had homes, a school, and a church. One six-year-old added a graveyard for animals and relatives. As if a cruel joke, a rainstorm came through and destroyed their handmade city. But this time, Leopold said, the kids and the therapists could work together to assess the damage and rebuild.

Other volunteers learned firsthand how children might speak in pictures before they can find any words. At the Reliant Center in Houston, a small group of local mothers began setting children up with art supplies. Their efforts grew into the Katrina's Kids Project, held in both the Reliant Center and the Houston Astrodome. Among the children was twelve-year-old Donald Expose, who told CNN that he escaped from the Lower Ninth Ward by swimming to a roof and waiting to be rescued. It wasn't until he started to draw that volunteers learned that his mother hadn't made it out. "I just started drawing, drawing it out of me," Expose said.

Arriving in Houston, I followed my directions to a school parking lot. I knew I was at the right place when I saw a banner that featured the traditional Mardi Gras colors of purple, gold, and green. It displayed a fleur-de-lis inside a star, which I later learned represented New Orleans inside the Lone Star State. Inside, hallways were decorated with positive-message posters with mottoes such as DREAM IT, DO IT, as well as kids' art that answered the question "Why do you love New Orleans?" with replies like "I loved my grandmother's house because it was underwater and I miss it."

Every single classroom in this school was filled with children from New Orleans who had been through some of the worst of it: the convention center and the Superdome, high water, hot days on a highway surrounded by dying people.

I found the class where the three art teachers were working. When I walked in, Geryll announced that I was from New Orleans. The kids loudly cheered. As I made my way to the front, a fourth grader stopped working on his personal power symbols long enough to tell me what he thought I needed to know.

"This is what I have to say," he said, speaking quickly, as if I might cut him off or turn away at any moment. "People were breaking inside stores but that was not bad. What they were doing it for was not bad. If you did not break into a store, you would die."

He talked about looting and survival, about his stay in the Astrodome, about his time in another school where they had served messed-up lunches and threw soda in children's faces, and about how he wants New Orleans back. I couldn't keep up with everything he was saying. Then he looked straight at me. "You like New Orleans?" he asked.

"Yeah, I like New Orleans a lot."

"Where are you from in New Orleans?"

"Uptown."

"Uptown's messed up, too."

"Yeah, parts of it are."

"I'm from the Florida projects."

"It's messed up?"

"Uh-huh. But I want to go back, me. I'm getting used to

Texas a little. Not as much killing people. They do kill people out here, though. I want to go back."

He picked up his work again, ending the conversation as quickly as he had begun it. He was drawing the sun, which was listed as the symbol for ideas.

New Orleans West College Prep was a kindergarten-through-eighth-grade public school run by a national charter school organization called KIPP, or the Knowledge Is Power Program. In the charter school movement, KIPP is generally well regarded for establishing urban schools that are highly structured and academically rigorous.

Four weeks before the flood, KIPP started its first school in New Orleans and staffed it with young recruits from the Teach for America program. When the hurricane hit, some of the teachers drove straight to Houston to help out at the Astrodome. At six thirty each evening, they set up educational games for the kids in the shelter. The first night, they were overwhelmed by the numbers; more teachers arrived to help out.

Some of the teachers wore KIPP T-shirts and were recognized by students from New Orleans. They conducted surveys of the cots and learned that about two dozen students from the New Orleans KIPP school were now in the Astrodome. "We walked around with a sign that said, NEW ORLEANS STUDENTS, NEW ORLEANS TEACHERS, NEW ORLEANS SCHOOL IN HOUSTON," recalled teacher Kyle Shaffer. "The response was amazing."

Houston ultimately received more survivors from the flooding than any other city in the country. By the first week of September, nearly twenty thousand New Orleans students were registered in Houston schools. But many parents were reluctant to send their children to school. They had already lost their community, their homes, their jobs, and everything they owned; many had lost family members. Now they were being asked to send their children away on strange buses into a new city.

"It was hard for them to trust," one teacher at New Orleans West told me. "The last time they got on a bus was when they left New Orleans for Houston, and one child might have gone one direction and then a mother ended up somewhere else."

At the same time, bad blood was emerging in some schools between Houston kids and New Orleans kids. There were fights. A report by the Associated Press quoted Gilbert Dawsey, a senior at Westbury High School, where three dozen evacuees and locals were arrested after brawling in the lunchroom. "Sometimes, you just can't stop how kids feel," Dawsey had said.

Deedrah Harp, a psychologist working in the Houston school district, told me she had learned what evacuee children had gone through when she saw a young boy's drawing. It depicted the view from his rooftop while he waited to be rescued. "It just struck me that this is ingrained in this child's memory, how it looked when his whole life was under water," she said.

Deedrah volunteered at the George R. Brown Convention Center after she had heard that evacuees were arriving. When she and a friend first arrived, they began sorting donated clothes. Then she heard someone at the volunteer desk say they were looking for mental health professionals. She began working with evacuees in the shelter, trying to get people just to talk about what they saw. The memories from children were among the most vivid. "Hearing it coming out of a child's mouth is different. Talking about the realities of being stuck on a bridge. The grossness of it, the heat, the flies, no bathrooms, no food, being scared to go to sleep because somebody might hurt your sister."

She asked them about what they were physically sensing and feeling. She told me what they talked about: "Being stuck on rooftops. The feeling of shingles underneath their feet. Remembering the things in the water that scared them. Touching things with their feet that they thought were dead bodies. If anything moved in the water—especially with young children—then that was a snake or a crocodile or something that was going to hurt them. And other memories. Tasting the salt of their tears."

Many of the young teachers at New Orleans West were barely out of college. Going through the hallways, I heard their voices giving loud instructions to students to walk in straight lines. In the classrooms, they delivered countdowns when each class and activity changed. At times, they sounded to my ears like drill sergeants. Yet I also felt the warmth and familiarity that clearly existed between teachers and students. Everyone there had been through the evacuation. That counted for a lot.

When New Orleans West opened its doors on October 3, about a hundred children showed up right away. The first weeks were rough. "They didn't have a school," Ruth Robbins said. "They had a bunch of really shaky kids."

Teachers grappled with the problem of how to teach subjects like math to children who were still mourning. At first, some kids would resist the lessons. "The teachers would use themselves as examples," Geryll Robbins said. "They'd be doing a math problem and the teacher would say, 'You might not like this, and I don't like the fact that my apartment is ruined, but it is. So let's just work with it.' I thought it was a really smart way of bringing up that there might be more than the math problem that was upsetting someone."

During the morning class I attended, I noticed that one student had brought in pictures from her grandfather's funeral. She had just returned from New Orleans. It was the first time she'd been back since the storm; she went to attend the funeral. She kept the photos with her during the entire lesson. "There's a complicated story behind every kid," Ruth told me.

One sixth-grade girl told her teachers she didn't want to go back to New Orleans because she didn't want to see dead bodies. "Her experience of New Orleans is that it's a graveyard to her," Geryll said. "I told her that I was just there. I said it was very sad to be in a city with no children. But it's no longer filled with water and death."

Another student arrived in class carrying a special issue of *Time* magazine that was filled with Katrina articles and photos. Ruth asked him about it. "He said, 'Yeah, I brought it in today.' And he just told me, 'When I read this, I learned I was poor. I liked my life. But now I know I was living poor.' He was in fifth grade."

When the art class ended, Ruth, Geryll, and Anne carried buckets of paint outside to work on a labyrinth they were painting onto the school's playground. In the center was a bouquet of handprints of the school's youngest children. While they worked outside, I found Principal Gary Robichaux in his office. He was printing out a map to a hotel that was still serving as home to one of the school's families. He also was preparing an order for 350 servings of jambalaya. The coming weekend, the school was sponsoring a resource fair for parents, and he'd discovered a restaurant that served pretty good jambalaya and gumbo.

Ruth had told me that the school sometimes felt like it could explode in grief at any moment. I told Gary about the boy who'd come up and started talking quickly to me about New Orleans and the looting and killing. In the beginning, Gary said, it didn't take much for emotions to heat up. Most of the teachers were white; most of the students were African

American. "There was a lot of distrust about us, even though we were from New Orleans. The theory that the levees were busted by the government, by white people, that was going around the school."

Gary walked from class to class; he stood at the front of each room and let the kids talk. The teachers led a series of workshops with the kids. They put up pictures of the Superdome and even wrote out a notorious quotation from Barbara Bush from the first week after the flood, the one about how evacuees in Houston were "underprivileged anyway" and "this is working very well for them." Kids were invited to write out and discuss their responses. Eventually, he said, the school was able to turn its focus back to academics.

Gary credited KIPP cofounder Mike Feinberg with the idea to start New Orleans West. Now, he said, the founders of the school were debating what to do for the next school year. At the upcoming parents' event, Gary planned to poll families to see who was planning on returning to New Orleans and who was staying in Houston. Gary's own house in Mid-City flooded. Still, he wanted to go back, and he wanted to bring the school with him.

One day Dan Jansen, the winner of the 1994 Olympic gold medal in speed skating, visited the third-, fourth-, and fifth-grade classes at New Orleans West. To prepare for the visit, students participated in a national Olympic Spirit Card Contest.

Children were asked to illustrate responses to the question, "What does Olympic spirit mean to you?"

No students from New Orleans West placed among the national winners of the contest. Most of the national finalists had incorporated drawings of flags and torches and the Olympic rings, and they wrote out statements about doing your best and overcoming obstacles. I looked through some of the New Orleans West drawings about Olympic spirit. A few were about accomplishing goals and keeping faith, and featured drawings of the Olympics. But for most kids, it was as if the word *spirit* was enough to ignite their simmering emotions about the flood and New Orleans.

"Spirit is home," wrote one student. "New Orleans is my home and I want to go back."

In another entry, a house was drawn inside a heart, and it was covered in a large blue block of floodwater.

I turned to a pink sheet of paper. The title across the top read, "Everyone Who Helps Me With My Spirit." There were pictures of smiling people and there was one long, breathless sentence: "I am glad that everyone who help me with my spirit is alive because if they didn't help me with my spirit I will be dead right now and me and my mother were separated because we went by my uncle's house the day before the hurricane and my mom was looking for us and she had found us on the Internet and that's how I have spirit in my soul and my people that save me have spirit in me."

The artist was Sariah Jones, age nine. After looking at the

cheerful drawing and the stark narrative, I asked school administrators if it would be possible to find out if Sariah and her family wanted to talk about her picture. Later that day, Sariah's mother, Rhoda Jones, called me and invited me to their new apartment on the west side of Houston.

I navigated the labyrinth of highways from New Orleans West to Rhoda's apartment. When I arrived, Sariah was in her bedroom, reading a children's book by Judy Blume. I recognized the title from my daughter's bookshelf. Rhoda's older daughter, Semaj, sat at the dining room table, working on math problems.

Rhoda started into her story right away. She told me about how, on the Saturday before the hurricane, she sent her two daughters and her oldest child, a sixteen-year-old son, to stay with her brother. He lived in the Iberville housing project, a three-story brick building that Rhoda thought would be safe. "I'll never do it again," she said. "We'll never separate again."

Rhoda worked in the basement at Charity Hospital, in medical records. She believed that she needed to stay in town to work, but when she called in on Tuesday, she gleaned enough information to figure out that she no longer had a job. She tried to get across Canal Street to check on her daughters but was stopped by the National Guard. So that Wednesday after the storm, she finally left with a friend and her family. She stayed at a series of shelters. She had lost her children.

A counselor with the Red Cross told her she had to keep

going. "I felt that I love my children so hard, I'd know if something was wrong. So that gave me comfort," she said. A month later, her son finally tracked down a cousin's phone number. The family reunited in Atlanta.

From the kitchen, Semaj was listening in on our conversation; Sariah came in from her bedroom to join in. Rhoda said that her brother walked her children through deep water to the convention center. There, her son stayed awake, cradling his sisters in his arms.

"When I was in the convention center, I cried a lot," Sariah said. "'I miss my mama, I miss my mama.' And I couldn't stop crying. Because I didn't know if she was still alive."

Rhoda's children finally made it out of New Orleans and moved from shelter to shelter. After meeting in the bus station in Atlanta, the family drove to a nearby house where they slept on air mattresses. "They talked," Rhoda said. "I listened."

"We almost drowned," Semaj said.

"Mama, when I tripped over that rock," said Sariah.

"I'm glad that part's over," Semaj said.

"I'm glad that part's over, too," said her mother.

Sariah talked about how all she had to eat at the convention center was candy. "They had beaucoup candy," she said. They also had dry noodles. Sariah's stomach started hurting. Her skin was covered in boils from the water.

I told Rhoda about the drawing, which she hadn't yet seen. I described the smiling people and what Sariah had written.

"You drew me?" Rhoda asked, then laughed. "What did I have on?"

They joked some more, then Rhoda sent both girls back to their homework. She checked on her son, Calvin, who was doing his work in a back room. Then she came back and sat on the couch. We talked about New Orleans and her old life there, and how her house filled with her entire family every Mardi Gras. "It was chaos," she said, laughing. She talked more about her children and about who was the better reader and who was better at math. As much as she misses home, she didn't think that they would move back.

"Those are two little girls," Rhoda said. "I don't want them to have their childhood taken away. I want them to have that."

Driving back to New Orleans on Interstate 10, I reversed the path that hundreds of thousands of New Orleanians took just three months earlier.

At Sugarcane Academy, we fought to keep our community together in the fall of 2005. Thanks to Paul Reynaud and the other teachers who agreed to improvise a school, we largely managed it. At New Orleans West, the kids came from communities across New Orleans that had been blown apart. They forged a new school community out of the broken shards of many schools.

In the months after we returned to New Orleans, the people who lived in homes that hadn't flooded talked a lot about survivor's guilt. We took drives to Lakeview or the Lower Ninth Ward or Chalmette, just to see things for ourselves. I later learned of a lesser-known condition called bystander's guilt. When we watched the flood on television, we cradled our own children while other kids were in danger. We looked for faces we knew in the crowds, but what could we do when we found someone we recognized?

It seemed that everyone I knew was battling feelings of powerlessness. I kept thinking of the boy in the town of Scott who asked every person returning to New Orleans to keep an eye out for his cat.

I returned from Houston to New Orleans with just a couple of weeks left at Sugarcane Academy. There, I visited with teacher Robin Delamatre. We talked about David Rae Morris's photos, and the art that the kids in Houston had made, and about taking Cecilia and Olivia to St. Bernard Parish. Olivia was one of Robin's students. I told Robin about how she was mad at the way Cecilia was responding to the sights of the Lower Ninth Ward and Chalmette. Robin compared it to a feeling she had when her sister's friend returned from Vietnam. He'd been shot, and then he'd gotten a tattoo of a spider around his wound. Robin's brother said it was cool; Robin was horrified at the reaction.

There is an awesomeness to these things, she said. Both kids and adults are amazed when they see a truck that has been carried by floodwater to the roof of a house. She said she had been thinking about what David Rae said about seeing beauty in the middle of the flood. Maybe that is an essential part of recovering. Just like painting slogans on your house or refrigerator, or even rebuilding a school that will last for just a few months.

I recalled standing on the street in front of Scott Jordan's house in Carencro, teaching Cecilia to ride a bicycle on the day the waters rose in New Orleans. I also remembered a story that Ruth Robbins told me about one of the families she had met in Houston. A little girl had walked in water up to her chest. Ruth asked her how that felt. "It was fun," said the girl. "I had my brother and my cousins and we had fun."

What made the difference was the girl's family, Ruth said. She wondered just what they said, how they had acted, what reserves they drew from, to keep up the spirits of their children.

CHAPTER 10

Pieces of broken sugarcane poked through the dirt. Mary Tutwiler steered off the paved road onto a muddy shoulder and parked her car.

"This is where I took the kids on the first field trip," she said. As my eyes adjusted in the moonlight, I could see only a few long stalks of cane remaining. It was nearing the end of December. The fields had been both battered by Hurricane Rita and burned in the seasonal harvest. We were now there to cut down any remaining sugarcane that could be found.

This week was Sugarcane Academy's graduation ceremony. On Tuesday, December 20, we would pass out stalks of cane along with diplomas.

Mary handed me a knife and we searched for any surviving long stalks. During peak growing season, the cane can get up to twenty feet high. "Around here, they say, 'You never know what happens down behind the cane,'" Mary said.

Now, in the humid stillness of a midnight in New Iberia, I thought about Paul Reynaud's lecture about Halloween, and how feelings of eeriness in a fresh-cut field once gave birth to harvest festivals and goblins and trick-or-treating.

As I stepped through the mud, I realized that this is what it must have felt like to be a seven-year-old in Paul's school. How many times in your life does what you see and learn and feel all come together in the same experience?

Mary remembered the day the school got its name. "Paul came back to the house one day and said that we voted, and it's going to be Sugarcane Academy," she said. "I said, 'Well, that sounds sort of formal.' He said, 'Yeah, driving through the sugarcane fields every day, that meant more to them than anything else.'"

As we searched out more surviving cane, we talked about the bayou and trips to Meche's Donut King and the future of New Orleans and how the kids were doing. "Another thing Paul said was that he hoped that this was going to be one of the greatest adventures of their whole lives," Mary said. "That they didn't need to wake up every morning with this sense that their lives were a nightmare. Because for the kids, it's always a new day.

"I think that was healthy for everyone," she said.

I drove east to New Orleans facing the rising sun. It now seemed like Sugarcane Academy might be my kids' last school in New Orleans. We had decided on a school in Evanston,

Illinois. Cecilia would start second grade there after Christmas break. We found a preschool for Miles. I was far from settled about our decision to leave our city, even as I went through the motions of preparing the house to be shown by our real-estate agent.

On the last week of November 2005, the New Orleans district had opened the doors to its first public school since the flood. More schools would open in January—including Lusher, where most of Sugarcane Academy's kids would return. As December wore on, Cecilia became more and more vocal about leaving. A sign in front of our house advertised that it was for sale. Cecilia and Olivia took to kicking it down whenever they passed it; it was a futile gesture. I didn't stop them.

One cold December morning, Lusher principal Kathy Reidlinger showed up for our morning meeting. "Good morning, boys and girls," she said to the children. Then, when the kids didn't stop talking, she repeated her greeting. The kids straightened up quickly. "Good morning, Miss Reidlinger," they said in unison. When the meeting was over, they ran to her for hugs. "I heard about those recesses," she said, smiling. "I think Mr. Reynaud's been spoiling you."

A few days later, the kids and teachers and parents all walked with their lunches to Lusher for a final field trip. The path to the school went through neighborhoods of dead bushes and brown lawns. We stepped carefully over sidewalk piles of busted computers and bathroom sinks. Search-and-rescue markings still decorated the buildings.

When the kids hit the playground, they scattered. I watched Ike Watson, a second grader, running across the lot. He ran like he was being chased, his arms pumping, his hair flying. Hearing the kids shriek, it was almost possible to suspend disbelief and imagine no hurricane, no levee break, no flood. Seeing them on the playground, it looked like August. But on one side, a truck for Coastal Insulation parked on top of a four-square court. Workers were rebuilding Paul's classroom.

Paul walked over to check on the progress; a pack of his former students followed him. Inside, ladders and new Sheetrock were propped against the walls. Tarps covered the bookshelves. Small, dusty chairs were stacked in the corners. Artwork from the beginning of the year still hung on the wall.

In the rest of the school, the windows were still covered with announcements for meetings that had been scheduled to take place in early September. I walked back outside with Paul and asked him if there was anything from the past few months in Sugarcane that he'd like to see take place in a regular school.

He told me about one day in New Iberia, when he and Megan Neelis had been walking with the kids to the library. Across the street was a large grotto that had been created in 1941. The kids pointed to it and asked if they could go see the cave.

"So we walked over there and the kids were running around the statues," Paul said. "A little bit farther downtown, someone had drawn a big historical timeline on a wall. So I said, 'Let's go down there.' When you got to the end of the timeline, which was present day, there were these two big red doors. Somebody left them open. So of course the kids went running in. And we were running in to get them out of there.

"There was a big fishpond in there. The kids were leaning over it, and then a lady came out to ask if the kids would like to feed the fish. Then she invited them in. It turns out it was an architectural firm, and she brought us in to show us all the models.

"That was sort of our experience in New Iberia," Paul said. "There's a time for planning, and then there are times when you let the plans go aside."

As the kids finished their lunches, Megan Neelis walked around the playground with a trash bag. We set out for the walk back to Loyola University. Teachers Michele Barbier and Lisa Sirgo were at the front of the line.

"This doesn't look very promising," Lisa said, realizing that their path was now blocked by a steam shovel. We were on the Tulane University campus. Nearby, a campus parking lot was lined with military Humvees. A security guard approached Lisa.

"You can't be doing this," the guard said. "Campus is closed."

We turned around to find another route. Word quickly spread from kid to kid that the police had stopped us. Somewhere in the few blocks between Lusher and Loyola University, we had gotten briefly entangled in the wilderness of post-Katrina New Orleans.

As we walked, I faded back and noticed that Yerema Yosipiv, Cecilia's first friend, was holding his older brother Pavlo's hand. Ahead of them, Eli Poche and Walker Huston were inventing new rules to the game of stepping on sidewalk cracks. Walker cradled his boxed lunch like it was a football and ran forward.

We finally reached Sugarcane Academy, our last field trip over.

One morning during the school's final week, Tami and I sat on the floor in the corner of Robin Delamatre's class. Robin wheeled a cart with a television to the front. She told the class how one of the Sugarcane students had been among the people trapped in Memorial Medical Center during the flood.

The events at Memorial were already shaping up to be a major controversy. The student's mother was a nurse at Memorial, working in a different section of the hospital than where euthanasia was claimed to have occurred. After the class heard a series of book reports, Robin asked the student to introduce the video. "This lady that my mom worked with put together pictures from all the people that were there with her," she said quietly.

Lisa turned off the lights. "So now we're at the end of school," she said. "And we're going to end today by going back to the beginning."

The film started with the words, "This is a tribute to our heroes . . ." Then the slide show began with pictures of water covering the parking garage, of a baby surrounded by machines, of doctors and nurses. Medical personnel posed in front of the dark water, smiling for the camera. These were the first hours after the storm, when they didn't know the water around them was rising.

Treadway Pediatrics, the office where Tami worked, was just a block and a half from Memorial. I used to meet Tami for lunch in the hospital cafeteria. A picture flashed on the screen that showed the neighborhood under water. For the first time, Tami saw her old office in the flood. "It's deeper than I thought," she whispered.

The pictures kept flashing, one after another. Busted-out windows, where workers tried to relieve the building of its stifling heat. Photos from the neonatal intensive care unit. A nurse. A mom and a dad. A baby. "Do you recognize those nurses?" I asked Tami. "Yeah," she said.

A piece of paper was taped to a window with HELP PLEASE written in red marker. People sat at a table, eating cold soup from cans. There were more smiles for the camera, but exhaustion now covered their faces. Another picture showed someone with wires on his body. "Maybe he was having a heart attack," Tami said.

Another picture was of hospital workers manually keeping a baby breathing. The children in the classroom didn't seem to know what was happening. The pictures kept flashing on the screen, one after another. A song by the band Green Day, "Wake Me Up When September Ends," played as the final photos flashed across the screen. A man waded in the water, holding on to a door. Air boats came down the same street that had been too deep for Danny Franklin and the other state troopers.

The screen showed the text of an e-mail that was dated August 30. "The kids are a little scared," it read.

The slide show ended with the report that the hospital was finally evacuated by the end of the week. Robin turned the lights on and made announcements about class journals. Students began to file out. I noticed that Anna Yosipiv, Yerema's older sister, and Claire Franklin had stopped by their classmate's desk. They were talking.

"Were you scared?" Claire asked.

The girl nodded. "Yeah, I was really scared," she said.

"Yeah," Claire said. "I was scared, too."

Kids filled an open area inside the Loyola communications building. It was ten thirty Tuesday morning. Graduation ceremonies were beginning. Parents clustered in the back of the room behind the children.

Mark Hughes stood up first, strumming his guitar. He launched into a medley of songs that he said he'd tried to write about the school. He sang a line from the Archies' "Sugar,

Sugar." Then he strummed the melody of "Jingle Bells" and sang new words:

A month or two ago
Our little school began
With Katrina refugees
In New Iberia

They took the school back home
And it began to grow
Now we're almost through this year
And we're sad to see it go

As the kids sang the refrain "Sugarcane Academy, it's the school for me," Claire Franklin stood behind a large brick pillar, nervously thumbing through a small stack of index cards on which she'd written a speech. When the song was over, it was her turn in front of her classmates. Tears filled her eyes. She handed the cards to Kiki Huston.

Kids in the crowd hushed each other. Kiki gave the cards to Georgia.

"Here is Claire's speech," Georgia said. "Sugarcane Academy has been a wonderful experience. I love being around little kids, I'm going to miss them so much. I think I'm going to start crying. I don't know what I would have done if I had to stay in my old school. I had to turn in a huge science project. You saved me.

"Special thanks to my teachers Michele Barbier and Robin Delamatre. Miss Barbier for having the patience with me in math and explaining things over and over and over and over."

The children laughed. Georgia turned to Claire; she had lost her place. "I'm getting confused here," she said. Claire put the cards in order for her.

"I'm not glad about the hurricane but I am glad about Sugarcane starting," Georgia continued reading. Claire walked forward and stood next to Georgia for the conclusion. "I thought about the song from *Mary Poppins,* a spoonful of sugar helps the medicine go down."

The kids applauded. Claire then took the cards back from Georgia and began reading out names. "Miss Sabrina, Miss Kahn, Miss Sorgo, Mr. Reynaud, Miss Mahoney, Miss Natalie, Miss Neelis, Miss Delamatre, Miss Barbier, Miss Kiki, Miss Georgia."

She looked up at her mother. "Cathy Franklin," she said.

Kiki presented gifts to the teachers. I stood up to tell the story about how the kids named the school. We gave Paul a large plastic bag that held a quilt that Tami's sister had made of the kids' New Iberia landscape drawings. Later, Paul would hang the quilt in the hall at Lusher.

The students' names were called. Paul had printed diplomas for each. Cecilia walked through the crowd and passed out the sections of sugarcane. The room filled with noise. It fell silent when Paul began to speak. We never imagined he'd make a speech. In fact, we'd never seen him talk in a room filled with adults.

"Sugarcane is over, but the thing I'd like to take back is the idea that this whole thing has been sort of an adventure," he said. "We didn't always know where we were going, and we didn't always know how we were going to get there. And sometimes it really felt kind of confusing and weird and strange. But really, that's kind of the way you grow, and that's the way you learn.

"So I hope that we keep that in our lives. That it's supposed to be an adventure and it's supposed to be . . ."

He stopped for a moment and shrugged. "It's supposed to be fun," he said.

EPILOGUE

~~~~~~

In the fall of 2005, Katrina evacuees and survivors created temporary schools such as Sugarcane Academy in New Iberia and New Orleans, the New Orleans West school in Houston, the Cajundome classroom in Lafayette, and the St. Bernard Unified School in St. Bernard Parish. In each school, teachers, parents, and children worked off-script, improvising solutions to a problem they never anticipated and hoped never to face again. Now, we face the greater challenge of creating lasting educational communities, places where the children of Katrina can heal and flourish. Like building flood protection for New Orleans, it's a sizable but not impossible task.

The lives of more than 372,000 Gulf Coast schoolchildren were turned upside down by the hurricanes and floods of August and September 2005. Nearly 70,000 of these children were from the public schools of New Orleans. By the end of 2005, six public schools had reopened in the city; this number grew to twenty by early 2006 and to more than fifty by the start of the school year. New Orleans was now a district like no other: It had become a patchwork of charter schools, state-run schools, and district schools. A massive educational experiment was under way.

At the same time, it wasn't hard to find groups of New Orleans kids who were still suffering, still in transition, and facing bleak prospects. In June 2006, *New York Times* reporter Shaila Dewan visited Renaissance Village, the FEMA trailer park in Baker, Louisiana. She encountered hundreds of children there. "All day they play video games, ride bikes or sit at a picnic table, watching men play horseshoes," she wrote. "They are not in school." Education experts have estimated that the evacuation might result in thousands of permanent dropouts overall. Sister Judith Brun, who worked with children at Renaissance Village, believed that the kids were neither engaged nor comforted at the local schools. "They all had terrible stories racing around in their heads," she told the *Times*. In November 2006, after a year of battling bureaucratic red tape, Rosie O'Donnell's For All Kids Foundation finally opened a six-building community center in the camp, with playground equipment and educational programs for children, and help with careers and homes for adults. O'Donnell devoted herself to building the center after she first saw the camp, where thousands of families where languishing. "It looked like an emergency trauma room for people who were emotionally dead," she told *Nightline*.

In the spring of 2006, the Children's Defense Fund published the report "Katrina's Children: A Call to Conscience and Action," based on visits to places where evacuated kids landed, including New Orleans West and Renaissance Village. "Education, after-school and counseling services in most trailer camps range from nonexistent to abysmally inadequate," the report charged. The Fund announced a "Call to Action for Katrina's Children," which advocated immediate emergency health—including mental health—services and educational support to make up for lost time.

Families returning to New Orleans in the fall of 2005 acted on the belief that rebuilding a school was crucial to rebuilding a community. In the Lower Ninth Ward, Dr. Martin Luther King Jr. Charter School for Science & Technology—historically one of the district's academic success stories—sat in ruins for months until the activist group Common Ground entered the building without permission and cleared out the debris. After a delayed opening of classes and a parent protest, the charter school finally opened at another location for 2006–2007, with plans to return to its old site the following school year. By September 2006, 90 percent of the faculty and more than two hundred of the original students had already returned to the school. "It's the only reason I came back," the head of one Ninth Ward family told the *Times-Picayune*.

Of the New Orleans West kids I met in Houston, only about 10 percent—around forty-five students—returned to New Orleans for the start of the 2006–2007 school year.

Principal Gary Robichaux closed down his Houston school and moved back to New Orleans to relaunch a charter school at McDonogh 15, which is located in the French Quarter. Another charter school was opened in Houston to serve the New Orleans families that remained; in the fall of 2006, about 150 kids attended classes at this new New Orleans West.

Jonathan Bertsch returned from Houston to become McDonogh 15's development director. His new office was in McDonogh 15's school library, where, in October 2006, boxes of new, FEMA-purchased computers sat ready to be unpacked. Jonathan was hopeful that New Orleans schools would be better equipped than before the storm, when shortages of basic supplies—like textbooks—were commonplace. Still, he said, kids in the city's new charter schools faced many uncertainties. National research has shown that charters generally don't perform as well as other public schools. One advantage to charters, Jonathan said, is that it's easier to close down a poorly performing school. But every time a school is closed, he added, there is the risk of creating new problems. "You have to ask, 'What's happening to the kids here? What's happening to the families?'"

Some New Orleans teachers and administrators chose to remain in the communities where they landed during the evacuation. Among these was Kim Hypolite, the former principal who found herself in the town of Scott, Louisiana, teaching a roomful of evacuated kids. She started the 2006–2007 school year with a new job as principal of a middle school in

Lafayette. Others made their way back to the city; Anne Crow, my daughter's former reading teacher whom I met again in the fall of 2005, returned to New Orleans to her old job. Keith Bartlett, who with Anne had started the classroom in the chaos of the Cajundome, also returned to New Orleans, where he became principal of Dibert Elementary. He told me that despite being well aware of the many problems reported in the city's new schools, he still had to be optimistic. "It's a really bumpy road, but I believe we're finally headed in the right direction," he said.

As for my family, we started out 2006 by bunking down in a renovated attic in Evanston, Illinois. Five months later, we sold our house in New Orleans and purchased a new home that was five blocks from our kids' new school. We found other evacuees in the Chicago area and at times struggled to make sense of the series of events that brought us there. On the night of my forty-third birthday, Miles started crying unexpectedly. "Why did we sell our old house in New Orleans?" he said through his tears. "I didn't want to sell that house."

We returned to New Orleans whenever we could—for Mardi Gras, for Jazz Fest, and, in the fall of 2006, for the wedding of two Sugarcane Academy parents, Jami Mitchell and Kat Walker.

The week before the wedding, the kids and I drove with Rich Collins for lunch and cake at Flour Power in Chalmette. Ronda DeForest told me that they were purchasing a new house just a few blocks away from their bakery. We also returned to Lusher for the before-school morning meeting. As we approached, Cecilia saw her friend Yerema Yosipiv. I pulled over to the curb and she jumped out. From the car, I could make out Yerema's first words to her: "I miss you."

Watching them walk to school, I wondered how often Yerema relived the week in September 2005 that he spent in a flooded New Orleans. His mother had recently sent me an e-mail with the details. The final night, she wrote, she and her husband and their three children all lay on their backs on a parking garage roof, with military helicopters flying over-head and the sounds of explosions coming from the direction of the Mississippi River. On Yerema's first day at Sugarcane Academy, he was too anxious to go into the classroom. Paul Reynaud and Megan Neelis brought Cecilia out into the cor-ridor to join him. They sat there quietly, the pair of seven-year-olds and their teachers. After a few minutes, they all walked into the classroom together.

Now, nearly a year later, Cecilia and Yerema were re-united on a crowded playground. Lusher's student population was a mix of new and old students; somehow, I noticed, the school had been able to rebuild a racially diverse student body. When music teacher Mark Hughes started singing a Chuck Berry song, kids of all colors stood up together to do their versions of the twist.

That afternoon, we found Paul Reynaud surrounded by kids in his repaired classroom, which already was as cluttered and comfortable as it had been before the flood. While I talked with Paul, Cecilia came up and sat across from him. She began imitating his every move. "She used to do this on the playground," he told me. She repeated his sentence. He raised his eyebrows in bemusement. She raised her eyebrows the same way.

The wedding was on a Sunday. Jami and Kat had each lost their spouses years earlier. We had gone out with Kat and her children one Mardi Gras morning when they sent away her husband's ashes in a handmade boat onto the Mississippi River. Now, we danced in honor of newfound happiness, while a brass band played.

"In New Orleans, the land of dreams," went the line in "Basin Street Blues." "You'll never know how nice it seems, or just how much it really means."

ACKNOWLEDGMENTS

Among the first calls I received after the flood was one from Tim Bent, who edited my first book, *The Kingdom of Zydeco*. Tim asked how my kids were doing; our conversation eventually led to this book. Thank you, Tim, for your vision and dedication to this project. Harcourt editors Jennifer Bassett and Jenna Johnson, and managing editor Sara Branch, brought focus and clarity to the work, in addition to catching my various errors. I received invaluable help on all fronts from my agent, Timothy Wager, who was always there in the clutch. Thank you to all.

Not only did Scott Jordan (along with his wife, Cindy, and sons Evan and Quinn) put up with me and my family during a two-month evacuation, Scott then helped me make sense of this book. Thank you also to Shala Carlson. To steal once more from E. B. White, it's not often that someone comes along who is a true friend and a good editor. You are both.

Thank you to Jerry and Sug Tisserand, and to Marilyn Tisserand and Denny Becker, for unflagging love and support. To Phyllis Reynolds, for shelter and chicken soup. To the neighbors of Kilbourne Circle in Carencro, for gifts and the occasional feast. To Mimi Boustany of St. Mary Early Learning Center, for providing attentive instruction for my son. To friends and family members far too numerous to mention here, for sustenance.

Portions of this book first appeared in the eleven-part series "Submerged," which was commissioned by the Association of Alternative Newsweeklies. Richard Karpel, president of the association, first reminded me that one way to respond to a disaster is to write. Thanks also to Ruth Hammond and Patty Calhoun for editing the series, and to the overworked editors of alternative weeklies across the country for supporting it.

In addition to my own reporting, I relied on coverage in the *Times-Picayune* and *Gambit Weekly* as I followed the devastation of the hurricane and the ongoing attempts to rebuild the city's public schools. Both newspapers are available online and I recommend them to anyone hoping to understand New Orleans' day-to-day struggles and triumphs.

Old and new friends—named and unnamed in these pages—shared their stories with me during trying times. If this book conveys just a fraction of what I witnessed of your love and courage, it will have done its job. Thank you to all the teachers, parents and children who created Sugarcane Academy, and special thanks to Kiki Huston, who kept it together when so much else was falling part.

Thank you to Cecilia and Miles, for your intelligence, humor and honesty. Thank you to Tami, best friend and lifelong love. Home is where the hearts are. Long live New Orleans.